"Two pastors from opposite sides of the Atlantic come together to share their stories of pastoring people in hard places. Mike McKinley and Mez McConnell care about what the Bible says, they care about people, and they care about the local church. Their stories communicate love, joy, humor, and wisdom. I pray that this convincing and compelling book encourages others to labor for the spread of the gospel where today there is no witness."

Mark Dever, Senior Pastor, Capitol Hill Baptist Church, Washington, DC; President, 9Marks

"Mez McConnell and Mike McKinley have written a book that we need. *Church in Hard Places* is timely and will instruct a generation serious about taking the gospel to and seeing the church planted in difficult contexts and situations. Those with the highest views of God and grace ought to be most passionate about seeing the church gathered in the hardest places. Mez and Mike spur us on to this task."

J. Ligon Duncan III, Chancellor and CEO, Reformed Theological Seminary, Jackson, Mississippi

"McConnell and McKinley have done us a great service in collaborating to write this accessible, passionate, and important book. Seldom have I read something with such a mixture of gospel ambition and hard-nosed realism. That's probably because it is written by practitioners rather than theorists. May God grant a plethora of such practitioners to be birthed by this book for the vital task of reaching those neither easily nor often reached."

Steve Timmis, Executive Director, Acts 29 Church Planting Network

"Finally—a book on this vital aspect of the gospel mission that is Bible-rich, gospel-centered, and church-focused! And it's written for the average Christian by two guys with skin in the game. *Church in Hard Places* is a gift to the church."

Jared C. Wilson, Director of Content Strategy, Midwestern Baptist Theological Seminary

"If your heart is moved with compassion for the weak and the suffering in the world, then you will want to pick up this book. But I must warn you, it's not the book you think you're getting. Instead, it's the very book you need to read. Mike McKinley and Mez McConnell argue that while it is heartless to ignore the needs of the weak and suffering, the greatest need they have is the same need we all have—to turn away from sin, embrace Christ, and grow in the grace and knowledge of Christ in a healthy fellowship of believers committed to one another under the faithful leadership of caring pastors who will equip the church for ongoing ministry. Apart from that, we are merely meeting temporal needs and offering no hope for a changed life now."

Juan R. Sanchez Jr., Senior Pastor, High Pointe Baptist Church, Austin, Texas

CHURCH IN HARD PLACES

Other 9Marks Books

The Compelling Community: Where God's Power Makes a Church Attractive, Mark Dever and Jamie Dunlop (2015)

The Pastor and Counseling: The Basics of Shepherding Members in Need, Jeremy Pierre and Deepak Reju (2015)

Why Trust the Bible?, Greg Gilbert (2015)

Who Is Jesus?, Greg Gilbert (2015)

Nine Marks of a Healthy Church, 3rd edition, Mark Dever (2013)

Finding Faithful Elders and Deacons, Thabiti M. Anyabwile (2012)

Am I Really a Christian?, Mike McKinley (2011)

What Is the Gospel?, Greg Gilbert (2010)

Biblical Theology in the Life of the Church: A Guide for Ministry, Michael Lawrence (2010)

Church Planting Is for Wimps: How God Uses Messed-up People to Plant Ordinary Churches That Do Extraordinary Things, Mike McKinley (2010)

It Is Well: Expositions on Substitutionary Atonement, Mark Dever and Michael Lawrence (2010)

What Does God Want of Us Anyway? A Quick Overview of the Whole Bible, Mark Dever (2010)

The Church and the Surprising Offense of God's Love: Reintroducing the Doctrines of Church Membership and Discipline, Jonathan Leeman (2010)

What Is a Healthy Church Member?, Thabiti M. Anyabwile (2008)

12 Challenges Churches Face, Mark Dever (2008)

The Gospel and Personal Evangelism, Mark Dever (2007)

What Is a Healthy Church?, Mark Dever (2007)

Building Healthy Churches
Edited by Mark Dever and Jonathan Leeman

Church Elders: How to Shepherd God's People Like Jesus, Jeramie Rinne (2014)

Evangelism: How the Whole Church Speaks of Jesus, J. Mack Stiles (2014)

Expositional Preaching: How We Speak God's Word Today, David R. Helm (2014)

The Gospel: How the Church Portrays the Beauty of Christ, Ray Ortlund (2014)

Sound Doctrine: How a Church Grows in the Love and Holiness of God, Bobby Jamieson (2013)

Church Discipline: How the Church Protects the Name of Jesus, Jonathan Leeman (2012)

Church Membership: How the World Knows Who Represents Jesus, Jonathan Leeman (2012)

CHURCH IN HARD PLACES

*How the Local Church Brings Life
to the Poor and Needy*

Mez McConnell and
Mike McKinley

Foreword by
Brian Fikkert

WHEATON, ILLINOIS

Church in Hard Places: How the Local Church Brings Life to the Poor and Needy
Copyright © 2016 by Mez McConnell and Mike McKinley
Published by Crossway
        1300 Crescent Street
        Wheaton, Illinois 60187

Cover Design: Mark Davis

Image Rights: Open Street Maps, Open Street Map contributors, OpenStreetMap.org

First printing 2016

Printed in the United States of America

Scripture quotations are from the ESV® Bible (The Holy Bible, English Standard Version®), copyright © 2001 by Crossway, a publishing ministry of Good News Publishers. Used by permission. All rights reserved.

All emphases in Scripture quotations have been added by the author.

Trade paperback ISBN: 978-1-4335-4904-5
ePub ISBN: 978-1-4335-4907-6
PDF ISBN: 978-1-4335-4905-2
Mobipocket ISBN: 978-1-4335-4906-9

Library of Congress Cataloging-in-Publication Data
McConnell, Mez.
Church in hard places : how the local church brings life to the poor and needy / Mez McConnell and Mike McKinley.
   pages cm.—(9Marks Books)
   Includes bibliographical references and index.
   ISBN 978-1-4335-4904-5 (tp)
   1. Church work with the poor. 2. City churches. I. Title.
BV639.P6M43   2016
261.8'325—dc23   2015018978

Crossway is a publishing ministry of Good News Publishers.

VP   26   25   24   23   22   21   20   19   18   17
   15   14   13   12   11   10   9   8   7   6   5   4

Contents

Series Preface

The 9Marks series of books is premised on two basic ideas. First, the local church is far more important to the Christian life than many Christians today perhaps realize. We at 9Marks believe that a healthy Christian is a healthy church member.

Second, local churches grow in life and vitality as they organize their lives around God's Word. God speaks. Churches should listen and follow. It's that simple. When a church listens and follows, it begins to look like the One it is following. It reflects his love and holiness. It displays his glory. A church will look like him as it listens to him. By this token, the reader might notice that all "9 marks," taken from Mark Dever's book, *Nine Marks of a Healthy Church* (Crossway, 3rd ed., 2013), begin with the Bible:

- expositional preaching;
- biblical theology;
- a biblical understanding of the gospel;
- a biblical understanding of conversion;
- a biblical understanding of evangelism;
- a biblical understanding of church membership;
- a biblical understanding of church discipline;
- a biblical understanding of discipleship and growth; and
- a biblical understanding of church leadership.

More can be said about what churches should do in order to be healthy, such as pray. But these nine practices are the ones that we believe are most often overlooked today (unlike prayer). So our basic message to churches is, don't look to the best business practices or the latest styles; look to God. Start by listening to God's Word again.

Out of this overall project comes the 9Marks series of books. These volumes intend to examine the nine marks more closely and from different angles. Some target pastors. Some target church members. Hopefully all will combine careful biblical examination, theological reflection, cultural consideration, corporate application, and even a bit of individual exhortation. The best Christian books are always both theological and practical.

It's our prayer that God will use this volume and the others to help prepare his bride, the church, with radiance and splendor for the day of his coming.

Foreword

One of the most significant trends of the past two decades has been the renewed commitment of evangelical Christians to fighting against poverty. An avalanche of books, conferences, and ministries is mobilizing and equipping Christians to heed the biblical mandate "to do justice, and to love kindness" (Mic. 6:8). This trend is truly exciting, since caring for the poor is one of the central tasks of Jesus Christ and his followers (Luke 7:18–23; 1 John 3:16–18).

Unfortunately, there has been a second trend as well: a declining commitment to the local church. Although this trend is widespread, it seems to be particularly pronounced among Christians who are the most passionate about social justice. Indeed, it is all too common to hear those who are working full time in poverty alleviation to express not just frustration but outright disdain for the local church. This trend is a profound tragedy with manifold implications, one of them being that the renewed efforts to help the poor are doomed to fail. Those are strong words, so let me explain.

Poverty is a profoundly complicated problem to solve. As we argued in the book *When Helping Hurts*, poverty is rooted in people's broken relationships with God, self, others, and the rest of creation. These relationships are broken due to a complex combination of the individual's own sin, exploitive people, systemic injustice, and demonic forces. There is a lot more going on than meets the eye, so the solutions need to move well beyond ladling soup, dispensing clothing, and handing out food stamps, as important as those activities can be. Indeed, the problem of poverty is so complex that it takes a miracle to eradicate it.

The good news of the gospel involves King Jesus using his power and authority to conquer the individual's own sin, the exploitive people, the systemic injustice, and the demonic forces that are at the root of poverty (Col. 1:15–20). It is King Jesus alone who can do all of this, so the poor—a group that includes all of us—need a profound encounter with him. By "encounter," I do not mean a one-time meeting. Rather, I mean a deep, organic connection to the very person of Jesus Christ, who saves individuals from their sins and ushers them into a new world in which there will be no more exploitive people, systemic injustice, or demonic forces . . . and no more poverty (John 17:20–23; Eph. 1:2–23; Rev. 21:1–4). The poor need to be united to King Jesus, and he is present—mysteriously but truly—in the church (Eph. 1:23).

It is simply impossible to alleviate poverty—in its fullest sense—apart from the local church.

Thus, if we want to alleviate poverty, we need churches in the "hard places" where the poor live. Unfortunately, many churches are located far from the poor, and those that are in close proximity are often unprepared for effective ministry. And that is where this book steps in.

Drawing upon their personal experiences both as poor people and as pastors of churches in "hard places," Mike McKinley and Mez McConnell provide practical advice for using the ordinary activities of the church—the preaching of the Word, prayer, accountability, and discipleship—to draw poor people into a transformative encounter with King Jesus. These "routine" activities work because God has ordained them to work! They are the primary techniques that God has established to draw people into a transformative relationship with King Jesus and to nurture them in that relationship. Hence, the authors are rightly passionate in their desire to keep these activities on center stage, rather than relegating them to a sideshow.

You might not agree with every word of this book. Indeed, I wish there were some things that were stated differently. But do not let that deter you. Mike and Mez are addressing a profoundly important—but increasingly overlooked—issue that is absolutely crucial for the advancement of the kingdom of God and for the alleviation of poverty: How can we plant thriving churches in hard places? As one who has dedicated a lifetime to addressing poverty, I cannot think of a more timely or important topic.

Brian Fikkert
Coauthor of *When Helping Hurts: How to Alleviate Poverty Without Hurting the Poor . . . and Yourself*
Founder and President of the Chalmers Center at Covenant College

Introduction

I (Mez) was fifteen years old when two things happened to me: one of my friends was stabbed to death in the street, and I became aware of the church for the first time. A local church hosted the funeral for my friend.

The church building was big, imposing almost, and built from bricks as red as my friend's blood as he choked to death on the way to the hospital. I'll never forget that church. It had arched wooden doors and reinforced steel protectors over stain-glassed windows. Its steeple loomed overhead. And it sat proudly in the middle of our council estate (Americans call them "housing projects"), surrounded by a sea of drab, gray, pebble-dashed terraced housing.

The church was open only when somebody died. Now somebody had died. I recall standing outside that building in the pouring rain as people carried my friend's coffin inside and committed him to a God none of us believed in. After that time, I associated churches with dead people.

Sometimes we would see the local minister walk up to the shops. We would usually throw stones and flick cigarette butts at him. Of course he always smiled. That's what ministers did, didn't they? Turning the other cheek and all that? Religion and that church in particular were irrelevant to us. We would talk about it only to mock it. The only thing that a church was good for was as shelter if you wanted to have a smoke out of the rain.

As I got older, our little estate got worse. In the late 1980s and early '90s, drugs began to take a serious hold on all of our lives. Lifelong friendships turned sour as greed took over. Houses grew steadily more derelict as decent people looked for a way to escape. Flowers and shrubs were replaced with motorbikes and car parts. Rows of houses were boarded up, with litter, weeds, and dog muck strewn about as a symbol of a deeper degeneration.

But I always remember that church building—red and proud with beautifully manicured grass, seemingly untouched by the disintegration of our lives. It was always empty and as dead to us as the graves surrounding it, but it was also a place of mystery to my friends and me. Years later when I was living in a crack den, dealing drugs and getting into trouble, I would stare out of my eighth-story window and look out at that building. Through my drug-induced haze I would wonder about God: Did he even exist? Did he care about people like me? I would wonder why the building was there with nobody in it. Maybe it was just there to tease us about how pathetic our lives were. I pondered on why they would build a place like that just for the dead. If you had told me then that the local church would save my life in years to come, I would have laughed at you. I was sure that the only time I would find myself in a church would be in a coffin. Thankfully, I was wrong.

Who Are We?

This is a book written by two men who genuinely believe that the Scriptures teach that the gospel is good news for the poor and needy, and that the church is for all people in all places whatever their status in life. Yes, many churches are dead, like the one that held the funeral for my friend. This is tragic. How critical it is, then, for those churches who are alive to the gospel to pursue the poor, the down-and-out, the hard-pressed! We write this in the hope that the Western church will get better at bringing light to the dark and neglected places too often found in their own backyards.

These are my own roots. I was abandoned at age two and raised in the foster system. By age sixteen I was on the streets full time. But God smashed my hard heart through the persistent witness of several Christians who visited me in prison, and he saved me. Since 1999, I have been a pastor/planter involved in full-time church ministry. In that time I have been an associate minister of a middle-class Baptist church, served as a youth pastor for an inner-city evangelical church, founded a street children's charity and planted a church for street children in one of northern Brazil's poorest cities, and overseen the revitalization of a church in one of Scotland's most deprived housing schemes, Niddrie Community Church. I am short, opinionated, passionate, and desperate to see this kind of work modeled and magnified throughout Scotland's housing schemes and the rest of the United Kingdom. I am more than happily married to Miriam and have two young girls.

What Is a Scheme?

A Scottish housing scheme is a cross between an American trailer park, an American urban housing project, and an American Indian reservation. Schemes were originally built as low-income housing for the "new" working class (after the Industrial Revolution), replacing many slum tenements. Today, they are a mixture of social housing and homeowners.

Mike McKinley is the lead pastor at a Sterling Park Baptist Church, a church revitalization in Virginia. Unlike me, Mike is tall and not really all that opinionated (except for matters relating to American football and punk rock music). He has written several books and is a member of the board for Radstock Ministries, an international network of church-planting churches. Mike and his wife, Karen, have five unusually good-looking kids (or so he tells me).

The great thing about writing this book together is that we come from completely different backgrounds and ministry experiences. Mike's church is in a wealthy suburb of Washington, DC, but Sterling Park Baptist has found fruitful ministry inroads among their neighborhood's homeless, the working poor, and illegal immigrants. I am presently pastoring a church in one of my country's toughest schemes and overseeing work in several others through 20schemes, the church planting ministry of our church. 20schemes exists to revitalize and plant gospel churches in Scotland's poorest communities. If everything goes according to plan, my group will plant churches in twenty other housing schemes in the next decade.

Our contexts are different. Mike works in a multicultural context, whereas I work in a comparatively monocultural context (although that is changing). Couple that with the cultural differences between Americans and Europeans, and we are an interesting mix.

However, both of us are committed to the gospel of the Lord Jesus Christ as the good news for a dying world. Both of us are committed to the local church as the platform and voice from which that news is proclaimed, where converts are discipled, and where we practice all the elements of church discipline and membership. We not only believe in their importance but we also assert their necessity for our work.

What Is a "Hard Place"?

We have decided to call this book *Church in Hard Places*, but recognize that we're using the term "hard" advisedly. In Brazil, I worked with children as young as five years old who sold chewing gum to make ends meet. When that failed—and it did—they were pushed into prostitution by unscrupulous adults. It was a horrendous life, and still is for untold millions. In some ways, yes, this is a "hard" place to minister.

But that's a one-dimensional assessment. I notice that when I tell stories like these to other pastors, they often pat me on the back and say something like, "Well done, mate. I couldn't do what you do. It sounds so hard." Don't get me wrong. I appreciate the sentiment, and it's nice to get a pat on the back once in a while. But here's my dilemma. In some ways, it is not hard at all. I would even say living and working among the poor can be very easy. Sometimes I feel like I need to come out officially as a pastoral fraud, and say to my friends pastoring in wealthier areas, "Well done to you, mate! Yours is the harder ministry."

When I listen to pastors battling away around Europe and the States in well-off areas, I break out in a cold sweat. How do you evangelize in an area where everybody has a decent paying job, a nice place to live, and possibly a car (or two) in the driveway? How do you break through the intellectual pride of a worldview that thinks religion is beneath them and that science has all the answers? How do you witness in an area where the average house price is more than $400,000? How do you talk to a guy who feels no need for Christ because he is distracted by his materialism? How do you make it work in an area filled with nice, law-abiding citizens, who don't cheat on their wives, beat their kids, and spend their evenings stoned on the sofa watching reality television? Now that's hard. In some ways, it's harder. Brutal even!

In the Scottish housing schemes where I now pastor, I can have a conversation about Jesus any day of the week. I can call a man a sinner, and he will probably agree. I rarely meet atheists among the poor. People also have more time to stop and chat. They have more of a sense of community, because they all live in close proximity. It is not a commuter culture. If you take the time to show an interest in them, they will come to an event even knowing you will preach at them. Of course, there are many who don't. But my point is that I operate within a culture that is comparatively open to the gospel. Any hostility here in Scotland is to the *church as an institution* because it is seen as a *posh person's club*. The hardest part of ministry comes in discipleship and discipline. In effect, you might say it is easier to get people in the front door. The real problem is in keeping the house tidy once everyone's inside.

Our point in all this is to say, yes, we're calling this book *Church in Hard Places* because it quickly communicates the idea that we are talking about planting, revitalizing, and growing churches that reach the economically and socially downtrodden. We have no desire to claim exclusivity on who has it toughest in terms of Christian ministry. Whoever we are, and wherever we find ourselves serving King Jesus, let's rejoice in the shared privilege we have.

Why This Book?

This, then, is a book that seeks to share our conviction that church work in these difficult places is necessary. Sure, there are plenty of lost people in wealthy places, and we are all in favor of more and better churches in those areas. But if you are born and live and die in a wealthy place in America or Scotland, you are far more likely to have access to some kind of gospel witness. The schemes of Scotland and the housing projects and trailer parks of America are filled with people who have the same relationship with the church that I had as a young man; they view it as a place to get an occasional handout, but not a place that has the words of life. The church in these kinds of places is largely absent. When it is not, it is usually so unhealthy that it becomes a net loss for the cause of Christ. That has to change.

So if you are a Christian wondering whether you might be able to help take the gospel to a hard place, we hope this book will excite you for what the Lord can do through ordinary believers in faithful churches in these communities. If you are a church leader and you want to mobilize your people to take the gospel into a hard place near you, this book will give you some practical "must-dos" and "don't dos" to help you along the way. If you are a church planter thinking about starting a new church in a poor community, this book will give you an idea about how to get started and what really matters most. Whoever you are, we hope this book inspires you to sacrifice your comfort in order to minister to the poor on your doorstep or further afield.

Part 1

THE GOSPEL IN HARD PLACES

1

What Is Poverty?

This is not a book about poverty. It is a book about starting, leading, and participating in churches that reach people on the margins of respectable society, people in "hard places." It is about being a part of a church that reaches poor people. So we thought it worthwhile to begin by thinking about what we mean by *poverty*.

Poverty can be a tricky thing to get your mind around. Our church's ministry brings me (Mike) into contact with different kinds of people in need. In one suburb nearby, we distribute food to Latin American immigrants who may not have the legal standing to pursue government assistance. In another suburb, we work with people living in a homeless shelter. In yet another, we work with "at-risk" immigrant teenagers who attend the local high school. By almost any account, these are the people that we would think of as "poor." But as we have grown to know the people in each of these groups, we realize that their experience of poverty is complicated.

I once spoke to a man who had recently come to our town from a very poor part of Central America. He was hungry and told me through an interpreter that he hadn't eaten a meal that day. As we talked, it became clear that this man and I had very different views of his economic condition. To my way of thinking, not eating for twenty-four hours would be about the worst thing that could happen. I have never been forced to go hungry against my will. For this man, it was nothing unusual. In fact, things had been much worse for him in his home country. His frustration was not primarily with his inability to find work to pay for his own expenses; he was upset that he wasn't earning enough money to send back to Central America to help provide for his family. As tough as things were for him at that moment, he was aware that he had access to more material resources than he had ever known in his life. He didn't think of himself as poor.

On the other hand, take the residents of the local homeless shelter. These people are American citizens. For the most part they speak English, understand the way American culture works, and have access to government assistance programs. They live at a standard far below what they expected for their lives. But if you step back for a moment, you can see that we need to give a little more thought to why we would describe them as "poor." After all, they have access to nutritious food, medical care, and indoor plumbing. They sleep in cramped quarters, but the shelter is warm in the winter and cool in the summer. They have cable TV, electric lights, and puzzles to keep away the boredom. If you were momentarily transported to the slums of New Delhi or to rural Zimbabwe, you might not think that the homeless back in Northern Virginia are that badly off. Their creature comforts would be envied.

Still, we know intuitively that these American homeless are poor. To deny it sounds like a cheap excuse to avoid caring and helping. After all, who of us in homes and steady jobs would want to trade places with them? My point is that poverty is more complicated than something that can be superficially captured in digits and dollar signs.

What Is Poverty?

When we think about poverty, Westerners normally think in terms of access to resources. We have a so-called "poverty line," an income threshold that determines who the government considers to be impoverished. Politicians and journalists weigh in on the various ways that poor people lack access to quality education, healthy food supplies, affordable housing, and adequate medical care. Public discourse on addressing the needs of the poor usually revolves around the best ways to help them secure those things that they lack.

In their outstanding book *When Helping Hurts*, authors Steve Corbett and Brian Fikkert analyze a study conducted by the World Bank that asked poor people to describe what it was like to be poor. And they found that the view that poor people have of their own poverty often goes much deeper than a list of the things that they lack. They tend to speak in terms of experiences like powerlessness, hopelessness, loss of meaning, and shame.[1] Merely providing resources will not relieve the deeper dimensions of poverty that these people experience.

Take, for example, people living in the housing schemes of Edinburgh, the ones where Mez works. Through government assistance, they may have access to medical care, housing, education, and the material resources they need to feed their families. But long-standing patterns of drug addiction, alcoholism, crime, and broken family structures combine to keep people in the schemes in cycles of poverty and misery. They don't need bread; they need an entirely new way of life.

For this reason, it is our conviction that churches that are

---

[1] *When Helping Hurts: How to Alleviate Poverty without Hurting the Poor . . . and Yourself* (Chicago: Moody, 2009), 49–52.

content to merely provide material assistance to needy people are missing an opportunity to minister to them at a deeper level. Certainly food and shelter are important. The point of the parable of the Good Samaritan still stands; indifference to someone in need is unchristian. But material resources and skills training alone will not address all of the needs poor people have.

The one unique thing that a local church has to offer to people mired in poverty is the gospel of Jesus Christ. The gospel is not a solution to poverty, at least not in the sense of resolving and removing all of the myriad problems that poor people face in their lives on this earth. But the gospel word is the message of God to people who are caught in the complex patterns of personal sin and systemic challenges that comprise poverty.

While those challenges may never change in this life (John 12:8), the gospel comes to a poor person with news of a loving God who did not withhold his own Son but gave him up freely for the salvation of sinners. The gospel comes to a poor person with the promise of the power of the Holy Spirit to change and sanctify us, breaking long-standing patterns of self-destructive behavior. The gospel comes to a poor person with a call to repent of the futile way of life handed down to him from his forefathers (1 Pet. 1:18). The gospel comes to a poor person with the message that he can be fabulously wealthy even if his economic circumstances stay the same (Rev. 2:9). The gospel comes to a poor person with a message of hope for a world that will be made new, where sickness and poverty and fear will be put away (Rev. 21:4). It is our conviction that the one thing the poor need most is the gospel message. Other things may be very important, but they are still secondary.

Three Pillars

If you imagine that this book is like a building, our conviction about the fundamental necessity of the gospel would be the foundation. But in addition to that foundation there are three other beliefs that serve as load-bearing pillars, holding up the rest of the structure.

1. The Gospel Will Spread

First, *the gospel is a message that must spread.* The New Testament shows over and over again that when the gospel message comes into the world, it comes with a powerful centrifugal force. Fulfilling the Lord's words in Acts 1:8, the message about his death and resurrection spreads out from its center in Jerusalem into Judea and Samaria and eventually into all the world. The outward movement of the gospel was so rapid and dramatic that merely thirty years after the resurrection of Christ, people had come to faith in Jesus in faraway places like Syria, Greece, Italy, Egypt, Northern Africa, and Persia. For this reason, Paul could write to the church at Colossae about "the word of the truth, the gospel, which has come to you, as indeed *in the whole world* it is bearing fruit and increasing—as it also does among you" (Col. 1:5–6).

This is the story of the book of Acts, where Luke tells us how the power of the Holy Spirit drove the gospel out from the center. The Christian message cannot be contained by the city of Jerusalem, the nation of Israel, or even the region of the Middle East. It must spread over the whole world. The very fact that two white guys from Scotland and America are writing this book is proof. The fact that you are a Christian who (probably) doesn't live in Jerusalem is proof. The gospel must go forward to all people (Matt. 28:18–20).

2. The Gospel Will Spread among the Poor

Second, we see in Scripture that while the gospel must go to all nations, *we should expect to see it spread particularly among the poor*. This is a matter of both historical reality and theological principle. It's true there were wealthy and powerful early converts (Theophilus and Lydia come to mind; also, see Phil. 4:22). James referred to rich people being present in the congregation (James 2:2). But on the whole, the church seems to have spread mostly to people who were not among the cultural elites. When a famine hit Jerusalem, the church there lacked the resources to survive on their own. When the churches of Macedonia took a collection for their brothers and sisters in Jerusalem, they could give only out of "their extreme poverty" (2 Cor. 8:2). As the apostle Paul wrote to the church at Corinth, "For consider your calling, brothers: not many of you were wise according to worldly standards, not many were powerful, not many were of noble birth" (1 Cor. 1:26).

But this spread of the gospel among the poor was not a mere accident of history or the product of powerful social forces, as if it could be explained simply by pointing out that poor people might be predisposed to embrace a message of hope. Instead, the Scriptures tell us that the message of Christianity found a home among the needy because of God's deliberate choice. As James wrote, "Listen, my beloved brothers, has not God chosen those who are poor in the world to be rich in faith and heirs of the kingdom, which he has promised to those who love him?" (James 2:5).

God is passionate about displaying his own glory. If he lavished his salvation primarily on the powerful, the wealthy, and the beautiful, it would seem like he was simply giving them what they had earned. But by showing favor to those who have nothing to offer back to him, God shows his greatness and confounds the world's system. Again, Paul told the Corinthians, "But God chose what is foolish in the world to shame the wise; God chose what is weak in the world to shame the strong; God chose what is low and despised in the world, even things that are not, to bring to nothing things that are, so that no human being might boast in the presence of God" (1 Cor. 1:27–29).

3. The Gospel Will Spread through the Local Church

The third pillar that undergirds this book is that *the spread of local churches is God's normal means for spreading the gospel.* The church is at the heart of God's saving plan. His love does not rest on a multitude of isolated individuals, but it calls out and creates a people who can now be called "God's people" (1 Pet. 2:9–10). And if the church is at the heart of God's purposes, then the local congregation has to be at the heart of the practice of mission. This is not to deny that individuals can spread the gospel without a connection to a local congregation. We mean simply to point out that such evangelism is misshapen.

God has designed the church to be the vehicle that takes his saving message to the world. Local churches teach the Word of God week in and week out, both to disciple believers and to evangelize unbelievers. They send missionaries and start new churches to take gospel proclamation into places that lack a gospel witness.

But it's important to recognize that the church is more than just a preaching point for the message about Jesus. It is itself a demonstration of the very gospel that it proclaims. The existence of the local church points to the power and reality of the gospel. It gives credibility and plausibility to the message of the gospel. In the words of the missiologist Lesslie Newbigin, the congregation is the hermeneutic of the gospel.[2] It's the way the world comes to understand the gospel message.

A local church is a community of the reconciled—those reconciled to God and (startlingly enough) to each other.

---

[2] *The Gospel in a Pluralist Society* (Grand Rapids, MI: Eerdmans, 1989), 222.

In the church, Jew and Gentile, ancient enemies, have been brought together as a display of God's wisdom and glory to the world. Reflecting on this fact in Ephesians 3:8–10, Paul writes, "To me, though I am the very least of all the saints, this grace was given, to preach to the Gentiles the unsearchable riches of Christ, and to bring to light for everyone what is the plan of the mystery hidden for ages in God who created all things, so that through the church the manifold wisdom of God might now be made known to the rulers and authorities in the heavenly places."

How will the universe know the wisdom of God? They will know it by the existence of the local church. As the people of the church love each other in ways that don't make sense to the world, they show that the gospel is true. As they love outsiders and welcome them in, the church demonstrates the power of the gospel to change hearts. As they spend their money and their time and their lives pursuing the spread of the gospel, they show what it looks like to have a life that is transformed, set free from the hopeless futility of life without God. The church proclaims the gospel and then lives out the radical, transforming truth of the gospel in its community. It demonstrates the gospel.

The unique way God has ordered local churches actually encourages the spread of the gospel. That is to say, God has particularly set up the church to accomplish the task of glorifying God by spreading his saving message. You see this in the leadership structure of the church: the ascended Jesus has given people to each congregation whose job it is "to equip the saints for the work of ministry" so that the body grows (Eph. 4:12; see also 4:11–16).

So in one sense, a church is a gathered group of believers that has been equipped by God-given leaders to take the gospel out to the world around them. The leaders of the church (in Paul's taxonomy, the apostles, prophets, evangelists, shepherds, and teachers) are given to the congregation in order that the saints might be equipped for the work of ministry. That's a large part of the job that Mez and I do as pastors, and that's the job description of all the other elders in our churches.

And as if that were not enough, the church is also indwelt and gifted by the Holy Spirit for the building up of the body. The Spirit has given the local church the right mix and varieties of gifts that it needs to carry out its work in the world. If the members of the church will exercise those gifts faithfully in the power of the Spirit, the church will accomplish its task.

Think about the task of evangelism. It makes a lot of individual Christians feel nervous and guilty. They know they should speak to others about Jesus but feel like they aren't good at it, and so they avoid it. But let's say you take four Christians and assign them the task of telling someone the good news:

- Alan is an outgoing person. He's good at meeting people and building friendships. But he's not great at sharing his faith clearly. He doesn't do a very good job answering questions and making the case for Christ.
- Carla is great at hospitality. She has people over to her house regularly and is good at making them feel comfortable and loved. She's not great at starting deep conversations, however.
- Raul is a real prayer warrior. He loves to pray for hours on end, asking the Lord to have mercy on lost people.
- Naomi is an introvert. She doesn't make friends quickly on her own, but if someone introduces her and breaks the ice, she's quite good at sharing Christ in a clear and effective way.

Chances are that on their own, those four people aren't going to evangelize anyone anytime soon. But if you put them together in a church and give them a corporate life together, suddenly there's a mixture of gifts and a blending of strengths that can make them a very potent team.[3]

Everywhere the New Testament assumes that these gifts have been given for and will be exercised in the context of a local church. Much evangelizing might be done alongside other church members, and what evangelizing you do on your own should not be done without the support, care, prayer, and encouragement of the local church behind you. And then when people are led to Christ, they must be incorporated into the life of a local congregation of believers where they will be helped to grow into maturity in Christ, joining in the life of the body.

Putting It All Together

So let's put it all together: if it is God's will that the poor and marginalized should be the recipients of his love and salvation, and if the normal way that poor people will hear of that love and salvation is through the witness of a local church, then it seems that Christian churches should invest themselves in establishing churches that will reach the places where poor people live. That might mean starting a new church where there currently is not one. It might mean working to see an unhealthy church in a needy place come back to life. Or it might mean leading a healthy church to embrace its responsibility to take the gospel to the poor. That's what this book is about. We are concerned that too many church leaders are looking for places where they are most likely to find success (defined as an established church with financial independence) rather than places that are most in need of gospel witnesses.

With that being said, we are not dogmatic about where you invest your efforts. Mez and I minister in very different contexts. He is passionate about mobilizing and training people to

---

[3] Tim Chester and Steve Timmis make this point well in *Total Church* (Wheaton, IL: Crossway, 2008), 59–60.

plant churches in the council estates of Scotland. I'm passionate about reaching Latin Americans in Northern Virginia. We don't pretend to be experts on everything about what you should be doing in your particular location, but we do have some practical experience (which is code for "made a lot of mistakes") with churches that reach poor and needy people. And so it's our hope that we can share some of those experiences and observations so that you might be challenged to work in churches that reach the hard places and poor people around you.

2

What Gospel
Do They Need?

Between my time church planting in Brazil and my work now in Edinburgh, I (Mez) have been on the receiving end of a lot of short-term missions teams. And while I appreciate the help, I have noticed over the years that a lot of well-meaning, Jesus-loving groups from the United Kingdom and United States will show up with their paintbrushes and hammers, but with no understanding of the gospel message they think they've come to proclaim.

Many young people speak as if the good news is all about them and their sense of self-worth. They may grasp elements such as the love of Jesus or the fact that he died on the cross, but it is rare to find an individual who can give a well-rounded and comprehensive declaration of the gospel message. It can feel like we have turned the greatest news in the history of the world into a therapeutic self-help system, wrapped in churchy-speak and popular psychobabble.

And just think: if that is true of people on short-term missions trips, who are likely to be among the more motivated Christians, how much more must that be true of the wider church!

The problem has become so bad that we now have to teach classes at my church, Niddrie Community, entitled "What Is the Gospel?" and "How to Give Your Testimony" *to visiting short-term teams*! We simply cannot assume that all so-called Christians coherently understand and can communicate the gospel. It is ironic and a little sad that people spend a lot of money and travel a long distance to help us share a message that they cannot explain.

So what exactly is the gospel? I realize that this might seem like an unnecessarily simple question to ask. After all, if you are thinking about helping the poor, you probably consider yourself to be a mature believer. But experience has taught us not to take anything for granted. Many people come to minister in poorer areas thinking they have the message down pat, but in reality they do not. And getting the message right makes all the difference when you are ministering to the poor (and everyone else!). A false or even an incomplete gospel is like a sugar pill. It might fool the patient into thinking he will get better, but it doesn't have the power to cure him.

God, Man, Christ, Response

The gospel is profound and beautiful enough to occupy the most brilliant scholar, but it is also simple enough for a child to understand and believe. The message is infinitely deep and wide, but we can summarize it under four headings.[1]

1. God

God is the infinite, eternal, holy Creator of all things. He alone is worthy of all praise, honor, and glory. His eyes are too pure to look upon evil (Hab. 1:13), and he will not leave sin unpunished (Ex. 34:7).

---

[1] For a fuller treatment of the message of the gospel, see Greg Gilbert's *What Is the Gospel?* (Wheaton, IL: Crossway, 2010).

The LORD reigns; let the peoples tremble!
>He sits enthroned upon the cherubim; let the earth quake!

The LORD is great in Zion;
>he is exalted over all the peoples.

Let them praise your great and awesome name!
>Holy is he!

The King in his might loves justice.
>You have established equity;

you have executed justice
>and righteousness in Jacob.

Exalt the LORD our God;
>worship at his footstool!
>Holy is he! (Ps. 99:1–5)

2. Man

God created men and women in his image. Humankind's highest purpose was to glorify God by reflecting his character and living a life of joyful, obedient worship. But all human beings fell in Adam (Rom. 5:12), and all people confirm their ancestor's decision by their willful rebellion against their Creator (Rom. 3:9–18).

Many people have a sliding scale when it comes to sin. So as long as they feel that they are not harming people or are not at the bad end of the spectrum, then they are going to be all right. But they are wrong. The Bible is clear that we don't start with a clean slate and then get judged on what we have done. We all start guilty. We are already condemned, however good we think we are or are not.

>And you were dead in the trespasses and sins in which you once walked, following the course of this world, following the prince of the power of the air, the spirit that is now at work in the sons of disobedience—among whom we all once lived in the passions of our flesh, carrying out the de-

sires of the body and the mind, and were by nature children of wrath, like the rest of mankind. (Eph. 2:1–3)

3. Christ

God the Father sent his Son to take on human flesh in order to save us. Jesus lived a life of perfect obedience to God and willingly gave up his life as a sacrifice for the sins of his people. On the cross Jesus stood in their place and bore their guilt and punishment, even becoming a curse for them (Gal. 3:13; 1 Pet. 2:24; 3:18). Three days after his crucifixion Jesus rose from the dead in victory over sin and death and has promised to return to judge the world and make all things new.

> For I delivered to you as of first importance what I also received: that Christ died for our sins in accordance with the Scriptures, that he was buried, that he was raised on the third day in accordance with the Scriptures. (1 Cor. 15:3–4)

4. Response

Sinners cannot hope to earn their own forgiveness by their good works. God commands all people everywhere to turn from their sins and put their trust in Jesus (Acts 17:30; 20:21). Following Jesus requires rejecting the priorities and loves that once captured our hearts (Luke 14:33).

> And calling the crowd to him with his disciples, he said to them, "If anyone would come after me, let him deny himself and take up his cross and follow me. For whoever would save his life will lose it, but whoever loses his life for my sake and the gospel's will save it." (Mark 8:34–35)

How the Gospel Applies

So we have covered the outline of the message. But this is not an academic exercise. Getting the gospel right is not merely a matter of theological precision. It has everything to do with the practical realities of ministry to needy people. In fact there can be no gospel ministry and ultimately no hope for sin-sick sufferers if we don't get the message right.

Every aspect of the gospel message mentioned above is exactly what people in the housing schemes of Scotland need to hear. Actually, it's the message that every human being needs to hear. But a lot of well-meaning Christians think that helping the needy requires some other approach.

But failing to understand each one of these four aspects of the gospel *is* the fundamental problem that needy people have. Let's walk through those four points again and stop to notice how they connect to the life and struggles of needy, broken people.

1. God

Let me tell you about Lachie. He is in his late thirties and has no experience of Christianity in the home. He grew up in the foster care system and is the product of a couple of decades of unsuccessful institutional reform. He was weaned on a diet of daytime TV talk shows, History Channel documentaries, a bit of spiritism, and a cocktail of conspiracy theories on the meaning of life. Lachie likes to talk about God, but usually when drunk or in some random home stoned out of his face.

In his lucid moments he isn't really sure if God exists. After all, science has disproved God's existence, right? If you ask him how science has done that, he isn't really sure. But he's confident it has something to do with evolution and some big bang.

But the one thing Lachie does know for sure is that if God does exist, God surely doesn't care about people like him. His life is proof of that fact. If God does exist, he must not like us all very much to leave us to suffer and let bad stuff happen. If

God does exist, then the best Lachie can hope for is to live for the moment and trust that God will forgive him later.

I have worked with both street children in Brazil and inner-city housing residents in Scotland. And in my experience, they are remarkably similar in their thinking about God. Both groups have an innate supernaturalistic worldview. They have no problem believing that some form of supernatural entity (or "god") exists. Make no mistake: they don't yearn for a relationship with God. The apostle Paul is clear that "the mind that is set on the flesh is hostile to God" (Rom. 8:7). But you won't find many intellectually convinced atheists in a housing scheme or on the streets of Brazil.

The issue is not that people don't believe in God. The problem lies with *the kind of god they believe in.*

- They view God as *irrelevant.* He is utterly disconnected from daily life; he's something to dust off for weddings, baptisms, and funerals. He's not really good for anything else.
- They view God as *disinterested.* Theoretically this god is capable of helping them; he's just not interested in doing it. They find it incredible that God could be "known" in any real sense of the word. They perceive that God (and the church) is only interested in posh people.
- They view God as *lenient.* To your average person in the schemes, God is not holy. He doesn't hate sin. He's contractually obligated to be a good guy. So you can be confident that he'll give you a pass on the last day. And if that's the case, then why should you worry about obeying him today? At the very least, there's not much urgency to please God with your life.

Because of so many wrong ideas about God, it is essential that we proclaim the character of God among the poor. We must present a God who is holy and who will hold them accountable, which is a direct attack on their morally *laissez faire* approach to life. We must present a God who can be known, and who in Christ has revealed himself perfectly to sinful people. This is a real kick against the cultural goads. This God is worthy of our service. He will replace self as the primary object of service and worship. When we know this God and are known by him, we gain a transforming amount of purpose and self-confidence in our lives.

Take Rob, a forty-something former heroin addict, career criminal, and thief. Rob did whatever he wanted, whenever he wanted, without any thought for the consequences. He stole, he lied, and he hurt people at will. To his way of thinking, there was no God and no point to life. Life was about survival of the fittest.

One day Rob heard about God, and his eyes were opened to see God's character: God's infinite holiness, perfect love, and implacable wrath against sin and sinners. That knowledge has transformed Rob's life. He now submits himself to his Creator and Judge. Now he understands that God's loving concern and personal care for him exist in harmony with God's holiness. As a result, Rob is no longer wandering around in a story with no script. He lives with purpose, hope, and direction. He no longer commits crime. He no longer is absent in his children's lives. He now lives responsibly as one who knows that his heavenly Father loves and cares for him and expects him to behave as a child of his.

All of this change in Rob's life, the kind of change that social programs aim to achieve (and rightly so), is due to a change in Rob's theology. Rob now understands what God is like, and that has made all of the difference.

Failing to present God's character faithfully and biblically has major ramifications in ministry to the poor, wherever they may be.

2. Man

Have you ever been with a person whose toddler is running riot around the house? The child is shouting and screaming and lighting the cat on fire when suddenly the frazzled mother turns to you apologetically and mumbles something about poor Johnny "being tired." Whatever. You know that Johnny is an ill-mannered brat, even though it would be impolite to say it out loud.

We all make excuses, mostly for ourselves. Well, these kinds of excuses are pandemic in many of our inner cities. There is a real victim mentality in housing schemes. It's like an open prison where all the convicts are innocent. "It's not my fault" could be the motto for most of the people in the scheme where I live and minister.

When I was a young man, I received a steady diet of counseling from therapists and social workers. They filled my head with the idea that I was a good person who had been put in bad circumstances. If I had had the same break as other people, they said, then I wouldn't be so angry and bitter at the world.

Time and again I run into this mind-set in my work. People have become powerless and paranoid as they relate to the world around them; they are powerless to change their circumstances and paranoid that the world is against them. And there's a strange dynamic when people become proud of their bad circumstances—as if they are the only ones who know what it is like to suffer. Everyone else is just getting by on what life has spoon-fed them.

Paul, a homeless drifter for twenty years, put it like this: "Before I understood myself from the Bible's point of view, I felt like a good guy who did bad things sometimes but only because I was trying to get things right. I viewed people as obstacles to get what I wanted, even my so-called friends."

Ricky, a twenty-year-old homeless, aggressive alcoholic, agrees: "I thought I was worthless, drifting toward death, depressed, with no meaning, and lying to myself that somehow it was all going to get better. But all I did was drink and gamble more. People around me only registered if they wore the right clothes and footwear. I didn't really care about them or what they were like. I only bothered if they could serve some purpose for me."

Things began to change in their lives, and in mine, only when the Bible confronted us with the awfulness of our sinful condition before a just and holy God. Romans 1:20 is clear on this matter: "For his invisible attributes, namely, his eternal power and divine nature, have been clearly perceived, ever since the creation of the world, in the things that have been made. So they are without excuse."

The Bible challenges us to own our sin and take responsibility for the things that we have done. Yes, we are all victims of sin to one degree or another; there is a place for compassion and mercy and sympathy. We should weep with those who weep and mourn with those who mourn. But the Bible never allows us to use the actions of others as an excuse for the things that we have done.

Anyone who wants to help people in needy areas must encourage them to see themselves not primarily as victims but as sinners and willful rebels. We do sinful things because we are sinful people living in rebellion against our Creator. God is angry at sin and sinners. His wrath is against us, and he doesn't grade on a curve.

This may be a bitter pill at first, but it is ultimately life-giving medicine. Just because my stepmother used my kidneys as a punching bag for most of my early childhood does not mean that I am any less culpable for my sinful, wicked rebellion against God. Putting your arm around my shoulder and just telling me that Jesus loves me and that everything is going to be all right is not doing me any favors. It is sending me to hell and robbing God of the glory that he is due.

This might sound harsh. But on the contrary, the pastoral effects are breathtaking. Paul, the homeless man mentioned above, now sees himself and the world differently. Listen to how he describes himself now: "I was the problem. The problem was my heart and my choices. Of course, bad stuff happened to me, but now that I see myself as God sees me, I am free to make different choices, be less bitter and more at peace with myself."

Ricky feels the same: "Understanding myself as a sinner has helped me to understand myself better. It has helped me to understand why I made foolish choices. I now see people differently. We're all in the same boat, even the posh people. Now instead of feeling bitter against those who have stuff I don't have, I feel sorry for them because they don't have Christ. I have a heart for people that was never there before."

Unless we help the poor to see themselves as the Bible does, we will ultimately leave them trapped and helpless like a hamster in a wheel. They will be destined to see themselves at the center of a world that is all about them and their problems. But when we help the poor to understand themselves as God sees them, we open up the door to real, deep, gospel transformation that goes far beyond our wildest imaginings.

3. Christ

Thankfully, the gospel message doesn't end with the goodness of God and the sinfulness of man. That wouldn't be good news. But in fact, God has done something about our awful condition. God sent his Son to live for us and die for us and rise again for us. Now there is a way for us to have a loving, reciprocal relationship with him. One day he will come again and make all things new, and we will enjoy unending fellowship together with all his saints and the heavenly host.

What will make my heart sing louder is the knowledge of what it cost him to do this for me. Knowing that Christ died for my sins brings with it a great emotional release. God really does care about the "little" people. It offers me real hope, a lifeline and a way out of the victim mentality trap. Those of us who have negative experiences of family life can cling to the greatest example of self-sacrificial love in the history of the universe.

As one friend puts it: "Jesus puts everything into perspective. I used to feel sorry for myself. I used to feel hard done by. I didn't really know my dad, and he left me even though I didn't do anything wrong. I used to get angry about that. But now God is my Father, and he loves me even though I still do wrong. And that gives me security. God won't walk away from me when the going gets tough. In fact, he sent his own Son to die a cruel death to sort me out."

It all seems so incomprehensible. So many people who were supposed to love us have done just the opposite. But here is someone who was supposed to be angry at us . . . dying on the cross for us! Not only that, but he pursued us when we were running from him. It's like having a big, protective brother who has your back now, except he's the King of the universe!

As a young man I grew up in countless care homes and foster families and abusive circumstances. Things happened to me, and I did things that left me guilty, shamed, and confused as a boy and then a young man. And frankly, I wanted revenge. I found that even early in my Christian life I was praying for many people responsible for my suffering to burn in hell.

Obviously, I had not really understood grace at that point. I had not really understood the atonement, that this newly found peace I had with God came at the cost of his own Son. But over time God opened my eyes to see that his supreme sacrifice meant that all of my sins had been dealt with; they were no longer the defining reality in my life. I was not allowed to wallow in them anymore.

That supreme act of forgiveness began to percolate into the way that I prayed for family members, old acquaintances, and foster parents. As the Spirit worked in my life, prayers for their damnation were replaced with tearful prayers for their salvation. Christ's great sacrifice so overwhelmed my soul with love that I was unable to keep up that barrage of hatred. His love conquered my hate and freed me from the cycle that had been the cause of my self-destruction for so long.

Being confronted with the almost incomprehensible beauty of Jesus's sacrifice forces us to review our place in the world, step away from self-pity, find freedom in his love, and through his Spirit find forgiveness and love even for those who have seriously damaged us. One friend, Stephen, compares it to "winning the spiritual lottery." Stephen reflects, "I used to dream of winning the lottery when I was a kid to pay back all the wrong things I had done. But in Jesus I have been forgiven, my sins have been paid for, and even though I can't pay people back, I can pray for their souls and hope they find what I have."

This is the Jesus that the poor need: a sin-bearing, atonement-making, guilt-cleansing, living Redeemer. A christ who merely affirms us as we are is a savior who doesn't actually save us from much of anything.

4. Response

We must do a lot of hard work in explaining true, biblical repentance when working with the poor (or anybody for that matter). Being sorry and repenting for sins are two completely different acts that produce two very different long-term fruits in people's lives.

Sin is grievous to God, separating us from him. Repentance is a *turning away* from that sin. The difficulty pastorally comes in the fact that repentance can look very different when dealing with broken and chaotic lives.

Take Innocencia, a thirteen-year-old street girl from northern Brazil. She had lived on the streets for most of her short life. Her parents abandoned her at five years old, and from the age of six onward she sold her body for sex to pay for food and to feed her glue habit. When we found her, she was in a mess. One of her arms had been crippled from a beating she took on the streets from a john, all of her teeth were missing, and she had been raped countless times.

One day, when she heard the life-transforming truth about God, her sinful position before him, and the good news of what Jesus had done, she wanted to repent on the spot. We prayed with her and trusted that she had made a genuine profession of faith.

Several days later we found Innocencia barely conscious in the streets, a bag of industrial-strength glue at her feet (incidentally, this glue is a far deadlier poison than heroin). My Brazilian team was devastated and angry; her repentance had seemed so genuine!

We got her to her feet, cleaned her up at our center, and spoke to her about the commitment she had made to Christ. "Oh, Pastor Mez," she said, "I do love Jesus. I have turned from my sin. Last night I turned a client down, and I am now only doing six bags a day instead of ten." She beamed at me with pride, and I felt chastened. Was I really expecting that she'd be a finished product on day one of conversion?

Repentance in the schemes of Scotland is not dissimilar, although not often as extreme. How about the man who comes to Christ, has three children by two different women, and wants to turn from his sinful, abusive past and be a proper father to his children? What does repentance look like for him? Well, one way or the other, it's not going to be simple and clean. For people in messy situations, repentance is going to involve making hard decisions and dealing with the consequences of a selfish and sinful lifestyle.

Sharon was a woman in her thirties who came from a terrible background. She had four children and all had been removed from her by the local authorities. She had served countless prison sentences for petty theft and drug offenses. She was loud and brash, and the leader of a gang of shoplifters in her local city center. She came to a drop-in center where I was volunteering and heard me explain the gospel as I shared what Christ had done in my life. She came to me with tears in her eyes and said, "I want Jesus in my life. I want to be changed like you have been." My heart went out to her.

I looked at her and said, "It comes at a great cost, and you have to know this. I had to turn my back on everything I knew, including my friends and even some family members in order to truly grow as a Christian. How you see me here today is ten years of painful growth. It doesn't happen overnight. Jesus asks us to count the cost before we agree to follow him. He doesn't want us to be fooled into thinking life will get easier. In fact, it will possibly get harder as friends reject us and misunderstand our motives for embracing this new life. Why don't you go away and think about that and come back tomorrow? If you think God is really calling you to repent and turn from your sins, then meet me here tomorrow at 10 a.m." I never heard from her again.

Did I do the right thing? I think so. I have done it many times since. Working with vulnerable people, the temptation is to push them into some form of commitment in their emotionally fragile states. It is easily done, and people from poorer backgrounds can be easily manipulated into following Jesus for a whole host of reasons. But genuine repentance is a work of God's Spirit, and we do people a huge disservice if we do not present to them the cost of following Christ.

One of my favorite questions to ask drug addicts who often sit in my office and ask me if they can "get saved" is: "What are you prepared to give up in order to follow Jesus Christ?" If the answer is not "everything," then they are not ready and they have not understood the gospel message. The usual answer is, "Mez, I will do anything." My response: "Anything? Are you sure? Okay, give me your mobile phone so I can take your SIM card and delete your dealer's numbers." Ninety-nine percent of the time they get up and walk out. If they can't pay that price, then they won't pay Christ's.

Five Reasons Why Getting the Gospel Right Is So Important

The gospel is good news, the best news in fact. And it is essential that we both get the message correct and also keep it in the proper place. If we get the message wrong, it's like taking corrupted medicine: it can't heal you. If we put other things in the gospel's priority of place, it's like buying a diamond engagement ring but forgetting to buy a diamond: we're left with a setting that beautifully displays . . . nothing. We must be willing to take the time to get the message right and to communicate it faithfully. Here are five reasons why:

1. Because Eternity Matters Most

The gospel addresses all of life, both this life and the one to come. Many young people who want to serve with us on a short-term basis at Niddrie Community Church are on fire for the poor and passionate about being "missional" and "breaking down barriers." But sadly they often unwittingly put the emphasis in the wrong place: racial reconciliation, social justice, or renewing the culture. The gospel message is not simply that Jesus loves you or that God would like to get you out of your current difficulties.

As we've said before, the biggest need in the schemes is not social or economic change. The biggest problem in the housing schemes is that people are alienated from a holy God because the stench of their sin is an offense to him. And so the people of the schemes need a real Lord and Savior who died and rose for them so that he can take away all of their sins and replace their stony, idolatrous hearts with worshipful hearts of flesh. No other message even begins to help.

To be clear, we are not opposed to helping people with their day-to-day physical problems. There may be situations where it would be positively wicked for a church not to help someone in physical need. But there must be a priority given to the gospel message; it has to come first. Poverty, violence, and injustice are real problems at a personal and societal level. But they are the symptoms of the spiritual disease we all carry around with us. Treating the symptoms is good and noble, but without the gospel cure, the patient will surely die. As we approach evangelism and outreach in our needy housing schemes, we must do it with this inside-out mentality.

James Montgomery Boice put it this way:

> The gospel is not just a new possibility for achieving joy and fullness in this life, as some seem to suggest. It is not just a solution to what were previously troublesome and frustrating problems. It is rather something much deeper that has been done, something relating to God, on the basis of which and only on the basis of which these other blessings of salvation follow. Packer says, "The gospel does bring us solutions to these problems, but it does so

by first solving . . . the deepest of all human problems, the problem of man's relation with his Maker; and unless we make it plain that the solution of these former problems depends on the settling of this latter one, we are misrepresenting the message and becoming false witnesses of God."[2]

2. Because People Are Saved in No Other Way

In Acts 4:12 we read, "And there is salvation in no one else, for there is no other name under heaven given among men by which we must be saved." If that is true, people must believe the true gospel in order to be saved and brought into a right relationship with God. There is salvation in no one else; there is no back-up plan. Those who think that turning up to a scheme and emptying a few trash cans and digging a few gardens is somehow going to transmit gospel truth by some form of spiritual osmosis are very wrong.

Faith comes through hearing (Rom. 10:17), so we proclaim Jesus's completed substitutionary work on behalf of sinners rather than offer a self-help program. Good works such as caring for the poor are a powerful sign to nonbelievers (1 Pet. 2:12), but in the book of Acts it is the Word of God that spreads and causes the explosive growth in the early church (e.g., Acts 6:7). Of course first-century believers were doing good works by feeding the poor, looking after the widows, and helping the elderly. But these things were by-products of a life lived for the glory of the gospel; they were not the gospel itself. People in our housing schemes will only be saved if they hear the gospel word proclaimed to them in a clear and comprehensible manner. There is no other way.

---

[2] James Montgomery Boice, *Foundations of the Christian Faith: A Comprehensive and Readable Theology* (Downers Grove, IL: InterVarsity Press, 1986), 319.

3. Because Otherwise We Will Give Up

If we don't have the gospel right, we can forget any type of serious church planting work in schemes. We must know what we're coming to do and the state of the people we're coming to serve. We cannot allow ourselves to be surprised and discouraged by the depth of human depravity. People in the housing schemes don't hide it as well as people in the suburbs do. Also, we cannot despair about whether there is a solution to the problems that people face. We need the full gospel, which tells us both the terrible truth about our sin and the glorious hope that we have in Christ. If we alter, soft sell, or pervert the gospel, the apostle Paul calls us accursed (Gal. 1:8), and we should not expect the favor of God on our work.

4. Because Real People Are Really Going to Hell

In Hebrews 9:27 we read: "It is appointed for man to die once, and after that comes judgment." In a similar line of thought, when asked about a tower that fell over and killed eighteen people, Jesus himself called people to repent or else perish for their sins (Luke 13:5). That might not seem like a very pastoral response to a question about people who had died tragically, but Jesus cared too much about the souls of his hearers to beat around the bush. Biblically speaking, there's something worse than poverty or low self-esteem: hell. It is real, eternal, and conscious. And so we have a duty to declare it boldly and fearfully.

All people are naturally under sin and children of wrath (Rom. 3:9; Eph. 2:3). Coming from a difficult background does not mitigate that reality in the least. In an age when much of the prevailing Christian thought about the poor concerns loving them and boosting their self-esteem, hell can seem like a bridge too far for many people. How often people come to the schemes with the idea that all people need is to be loved or, worse yet, to learn how to love themselves! If that's your diagnosis of the problem, then you will never tell people about the reality of judgment and eternal punishment. After all, that is not exactly a boost to the old self-esteem levels!

But if the Bible is accurate, then you must believe that in their natural state, men and women are bound for hell. Hebrews 9:27 is either correct or not; people will either stand before God in judgment or they will not. There is no hermeneutical juggling that can arrive at a middle ground on this one. In light of that, the most loving thing we can do is to warn them about their eternal fate.

Some people who visit the schemes use the phrase "hell on earth" to describe what they find there, but in fact that only goes to show that they have no idea what hell is really like. Consider the following Scriptures:

> In that place there will be weeping and gnashing of teeth. (Matt. 8:12)

> Then he will say to those on his left, "Depart from me, you cursed, into the eternal fire prepared for the devil and his angels." (Matt. 25:41)

> But as for the cowardly, the faithless, the detestable, as for murderers, the sexually immoral, sorcerers, idolaters, and all liars, their portion will be in the lake that burns with fire and sulfur, which is the second death. (Rev. 21:8)

The life of every human being goes on forever. What matters most is where it gets spent. I fear that most of the church's evangelistic lethargy is due to the fact that we do not take the doctrine of hell seriously enough to care. The most loving thing we can do for people in the schemes is not to help them with their electricity bill, or help them find work, or clean them up, or give them a bed, or help with their drug habit. The most loving thing we can do for our fellow human beings is to proclaim to them the reality and seriousness of hell, no matter what they might think of us afterward. That is a selfless act of love.

Part of the truth about God will not do. The Bible describes God in many ways: he is angry at sin, he loves sinners, he hates and weeps and rejoices. He judges sin and sinners but he also forgives and justifies the genuinely repentant. We don't preach a purely angry God any more than we preach God as a cosmic Santa Claus. We preach a full gospel, not because people deserve it, but because Christ's ultimate, loving, selfless, justifying, sanctifying, and cosmic act of grace merits it. We preach to them because we love him who first loved us.

5. Because of the Glory of God

The gospel is ultimately about the glory of God (notice in 2 Cor. 4:4 Paul calls it "the gospel of the glory of Christ"). God chose to save sinners in a way that shows himself to be both just and forgiving (Rom. 3:26). He chose to redeem his people in a way that stirs up eternal praise in their hearts (Rev. 5:12). He chose to accomplish all of this in a way that magnified his wisdom while nullifying and frustrating the so-called wisdom of the powers of the world in rebellion against him (1 Cor. 1:21).

Do we presume to know better than God? Do we have a better, more glorifying gospel than the one that God planned from all eternity and executed in time? A man-centered gospel (God loves you so much, won't you please choose him?) glorifies sinners. Without a message of judgment, God seems unjust and permissive, not glorious. Without a call to repentance and holiness, Jesus is proclaimed as a savior who is impotent to defeat sin in the lives of his people (contrast 1 John 3:8).

God wants to save sinners in the housing schemes of Scotland and the immigrant neighborhoods of Northern Virginia. That conviction underlies everything that is to come in this book. But he will not do it through any other means than the glorious gospel of his Son. He will not share his glory, so no half-gospel or watered-down message will do.

Conclusion

Fourteen years ago a small band of young Christians turned up outside a community center on the streets of Swindon and told me I was going to hell. They then told me what I needed to do to avoid it. Hear the good news, receive the good news, repent, believe, and be baptized. I didn't want to hear it. But four years and lots of pain, anger, and some genuine repentance later, I was saved by the merciful grace of God. I write these words as a pastor today because those Christians (literally) took their life in their hands and gave it to me "straight up." That is what God asks of us. That is our primary task if we want to reach and help people in need.

3

Does Doctrine Matter?

A few years ago I (Mike) sat down for coffee with an old college friend and listened to him explain how his view of ministry had changed since we had been students. He was now in leadership over college ministries on a number of local university campuses, and he was explaining their decision not to be as "cross-centered" (his word) as we had both been fifteen years earlier: "You know, Mike, we prefer not to be so . . . *doctrinal*. The cross is important, to be sure. But we don't want to get stuck in sixteenth-century arguments over the atonement. After all, Jesus used a lot of different images to describe his salvation, things like a mustard seed growing. We want to spread the kingdom of God by proclaiming good news to the poor and freedom to the captives. There's good work to be done, so we can't get bogged down in theology."

Leaving aside for a moment whether the apostle Paul would agree with my friend's priorities (since he declared to the Corinthians that he wanted to know nothing among them but the kingdom of God spreading like a mustard seed . . . oh wait, never mind [1 Cor. 2:2]), what about his larger point? His position is not without merit.

Let's say, for the sake of illustration, that you are on a ship sailing to a faraway town to warn the people of impending doom. If you don't get there in time, everyone dies. Needless to say, you want your ship to sail as fast as possible. You avoid any excess cargo that might slow your progress. You don't waste time worrying about clean decks or polished brass. The urgency of the task requires you to operate with efficiency and leanness.

People like my friend argue that the urgency of the Christian mission requires us to trim our theological sails and jettison the heavy freight of doctrinal precision. Such freight yields only bickering and in-fighting between people who should work together. If people are suffering, the poor are oppressed, and the captives are bound, why write books and hold conferences and argue about the meaning of a few words?

There is a point here. The church would probably be better off if Christians spent less time bickering on the Internet about infralapsarianism and more time talking to their neighbors about Jesus. But that does not mean that churches looking to reach the poor and needy should jettison convictions and conversations about theology.

Doctrine is not freight on the ship. It's the hull and mast.

A church's doctrine determines the character and quality of its witness. Its theology shapes its goals and the way it tries to achieve those goals. Consider Jesus's words to his disciples in the Great Commission:

> And Jesus came and said to them, "All authority in heaven and on earth has been given to me. Go therefore and make disciples of all nations, baptizing them in the name of the Father and of the Son and of the Holy Spirit, teaching them to observe all that I have commanded you. And behold, I am with you always, to the end of the age." (Matt. 28:18–20)

Jesus commands the disciples to go and make disciples, which involves two steps:

- First, they are to baptize the nations in the name of the Father, Son, and Holy Spirit. Discipleship begins with men and women coming to repentance and faith in the Lord Jesus through the proclamation of the gospel. Baptism is the culmination of that initial stage of disciple making.
- Second, they are to teach them to obey all that he has commanded. This is the ongoing process of discipleship, as the newly baptized convert learns what it means to live a life that is pleasing to God.

So the question for this chapter is this: do these two aspects of disciple making require churches to know and teach doctrine? Can we achieve those twin goals simply by demonstrating the love of Christ and working to renew our communities through acts of service? It sure seems unlikely.

Instead, what we see in the New Testament is that theology is essential to every aspect of a church's life. Let's consider four arenas in which this is the case: salvation, sanctification, leadership, and evangelism.

Salvation Requires Doctrine

Critics of doctrinal necessity sometimes snidely remark that surely God is not going to open up people's heads on the last day to ensure the right doctrinal formulas are inside. No, probably not. But he will ask them something like, "Were you trusting *me*? The real and true me, and not a made-up version of me?" In other words, God is very much interested in whether we are trusting in certain truths, because with God doctrinal truth is personal truth.

To experience Christ's salvation, a person must believe and

trust the truths about the *real* God that we outlined in the last chapter:

- That he is the Creator to whom we owe our lives (Gen. 1:26–28).
- That he is holy and just and must punish our sin through damnation (Rom. 3:23).
- That he is merciful and compassionate and so sent Jesus, the God-man, to die on the cross for sin and rise again (Rom. 3:21–26; 4:25).
- That he calls us to turn from our sins and trust in Christ (John 3:16; Acts 17:30).

Simply put, if someone has not turned with his or her whole heart to God and trusted in these glorious truths about God, he or she cannot be saved (Rom. 10:13–17). Doctrine is required for salvation![1]

This is why, when the apostles went about making disciples, they did not shy away from preaching doctrinal messages. Look at all the doctrinal topics they and others covered for the unbelieving crowds in the book of Acts:[2]

- The Holy Spirit (2:14–21)
- The sovereign providence of God (2:23; 17:26)
- The resurrection of Christ (2:24–32; 3:15)
- The crucifixion of Christ (8:32–35; 13:28–29)
- The way the Old Testament points to Jesus (3:22–24; 7:2–53; 28:23)
- The reality of the coming judgment (10:42; 17:31; 24:25)
- The exclusivity of Christ (4:12; 19:26)
- God the Creator (14:15–17; 17:24)

---

[1] For a more detailed discussion on the necessity of belief in true doctrine for salvation, see chapter 3 of Mike's book *Am I Really a Christian?* (Wheaton, IL: Crossway, 2011).

[2] We have listed only a sampling of the possible citations from the book of Acts. If you are looking for it, doctrine is stuffed into every corner of the evangelistic preaching of the apostles and early church leaders.

- God's self-sufficiency (17:24–25)
- The kingdom of God (19:8; 28:23)

The apostles understood that in order for unbelievers to come to repentance and faith in Christ, they needed to understand certain truths about God and his salvation through Christ.

In fact, when Jesus appears to a discouraged and dispirited Paul in a dream, he tells him: "Take courage, for as you have testified to the facts about me in Jerusalem, so you must testify also in Rome" (Acts 23:11). Jesus summarizes Paul's entire evangelistic ministry, both to Jews and Gentiles, as *testifying to the facts about him.* That's what Paul did; he went from town to town conveying facts about who Jesus was and what he did.

It is hard to reconcile this picture of the church's evangelistic task with the claim that our witness should be driven primarily by acts of love and mercy toward the needy. The fact is, the world can watch Christians ladle soup or paint over graffiti for a thousand years, and they'll never come to the conclusion the Jesus died for their sins and rose again. We must open our mouths and speak the content of the gospel to the world, or no one will be saved.

Sanctification Requires Doctrine

Some might be tempted to believe that a person needs a basic amount of doctrine to *become* a Christian, but that most of what we call "theology" or "doctrine" is unnecessary to grow as a Christian. Sure, if you have a temperament that enjoys contemplating complicated concepts and arguing with strangers online, dig deeper. But for the rest of us, we need to get about the business of living like Jesus in our communities.

But it turns out that the authors of Scripture don't share that point of view. Time and again, the Bible anchors right actions and behaviors and attitudes for God's people in right doctrine. Look at these examples:

- *The Ten Commandments.* This is the granddaddy of them all—the Big List of How to Live. Yet what comes immediately before these instructions for godly living? A piece of theology: "I am the LORD your God, who brought you out of the land of Egypt, out of the house of slavery" (Ex. 20:2). Why should the Israelites have no other gods? Because the Lord delivered them from slavery.

- *Love your enemies.* Here's a command that gets our gospel transformation juices flowing! But notice that Jesus grounds such active love in theology: "Love your enemies and pray for those who persecute you, so that you may be sons of your Father who is in heaven. For he makes his sun rise on the evil and on the good, and sends rain on the just and on the unjust" (Matt. 5:44–45). Why should we love our enemies? Because God, our Father, is an enemy-loving God!

- *Be holy.* Christians are supposed to be holy. Why? Again, an apostle takes us to doctrine: "As obedient children, do not be conformed to the passions of your former ignorance, but as he who called you is holy, you also be holy in all your conduct" (1 Pet. 1:14–15). We don't conform to the passions that once ruled us because of the holiness of God.

- *The letters of Paul.* Finally, the structure of Paul's letters grounds commands in truths. Paul wants the recipients of his letters to present their bodies as living sacrifices (Rom. 12:1), to put on the new self (Eph. 4:24), and to walk in Christ Jesus (Col. 2:6). But such commands come only after lengthy discussions of doctrine. Paul gives these churches an education in things like justification and glorification, typology and federal headship (Rom. 5:12–17; 8:30), election and predestination (Eph. 1:4–6), the depravity of man (Eph. 2:1–3), and christology (Col. 1:15–20).

Christian obedience, including sacrificially reaching out to the needy, must be anchored in and motivated by the character and activity of God. Remove the anchor and you might stay in the same spot for a little while, but soon the wind and waves will push you away. Such sacrificial activity will soon stop.

The more we know about God, the more we will be moved to obedience. How many people have prayed a prayer in a church or mission hall but then never moved on because they weren't taught some of the real, doctrinal meat of the faith? How many Christians are stuck in patterns of selfishness and laziness and sin because they haven't been challenged to consider the character of God and its implications for their life?

But Hold On . . .

One objection that I hear from time to time is that poor communities typically have less access to quality education, which means the people in those communities do not have the necessary tools to learn doctrine. If people are not living in an environment where reading and study is normal, or if illiteracy is widespread, you cannot teach them complicated theological concepts. If you try, you will shoot over their heads and lose their interest.

Honestly, such attitudes strike me as paternalistic and condescending. Poor people are poor, but they are not stupid. They are just as capable of understanding the character and ways of God as anyone else. Paul didn't write his letters to the faculty of a seminary. His readers were generally not wealthy, privileged, or well-educated. And the Israelites leaving Egypt didn't have advanced degrees in theology, but God didn't hesitate to tell them all kinds of in-depth and complicated things about himself.

Poor people can grasp deep truths. I have seen that this is

true in the church I serve in the States, and I saw the same thing at work in Mez's context in Edinburgh.

Consider Gordon. He is in his early forties. He never finished high school and had never read a book in his life before his conversion. He had no prior experience with church or Christianity. He was literate, but only at a level that let him read a newspaper. When Gordon first came to Mez's church, he said that the teaching was over his head. I'll let him explain it in his words:

> Before I got saved, I couldn't understand what was being said in the Bible. Now it's like it calls my name and draws me to it. I think that's the Holy Spirit. I find myself thinking about the deep questions of life in a way I never did before. I just want to read all the time. Even though I got lost with the big theological words, I was determined to learn them. I wanted to love God more. I wanted to know him more. What helped was having good people around me who explained everything to me without patronizing me. At school, if a thing were too hard then I would just give up. Now, even though learning some of this stuff hurts my head, I have learned to persevere and have patience with myself.

Prior to faith in Christ, Gordon couldn't hold down a full-time job. He was addicted to hard drugs and lived a chaotic life. He says he couldn't sit still for more than two minutes. Now he sits and listens to a forty-minute sermon without any trouble and he loves studying the Bible at every opportunity.

We shouldn't sell people short because they aren't educated or well-read. Granted, you will need to adjust your pedagogical methods if you are working with people who are completely illiterate or mentally impaired. But all good teachers adjust their material to the level of their hearers. In our experience, we have yet to come across a doctrinal topic that was simply too complicated for needy people to understand. If you teach doctrine clearly and well, relying on the Holy Spirit, God's people will want to learn it and grow from it.

Leadership Requires Doctrine

The New Testament clearly teaches that a certain degree of doctrinal proficiency is required for church leadership. Leaders are required to protect the congregation from false doctrine and theological error.

- An elder, says Paul, "must hold firm to the trustworthy word as taught, so that he may be able to give instruction in sound doctrine and also to rebuke those who contradict it" (Titus 1:9).
- And Timothy, he said, should "remain at Ephesus so that you may charge certain persons not to teach any different doctrine, nor to devote themselves to myths and endless genealogies, which promote speculations rather than the stewardship from God that is by faith" (1 Tim. 1:3–4).
- And not just Timothy but all of a church's leaders: "And the Lord's servant must not be quarrelsome but kind to everyone, able to teach, patiently enduring evil, correcting his opponents with gentleness. God may perhaps grant them repentance leading to a knowledge of the truth, and they may come to their senses and escape from the snare of the devil, after being captured by him to do his will" (2 Tim. 2:24–26).

True doctrine is life giving and sanctifying; false teaching destroys the soul (see Rev. 2:20–23). So Paul warned the Ephesian elders that "fierce wolves" would come in among the flock and speak "twisted things." Therefore, Paul instructed them, "Pay careful attention to yourselves and to all the flock, in which the Holy Spirit has made you overseers, to care for the church of God, which he obtained with his own blood" (Acts 20:28). A church without leaders who clearly teach sound doctrine is like a wounded antelope trailing behind the herd. A spiritual predator will pick it off.

We do pray for a movement of pastors and church planters who will work in difficult places. But it is easy to get swept up in the intensity and energy of starting something new or doing something challenging. People in poor and needy areas don't primarily need leaders who are entrepreneurial or creative; they need church leaders who devote themselves to teaching the faith that was once for all delivered to the saints (Jude 3).

Evangelism Requires Doctrine

Doctrine forms the content of our evangelism. But doctrine also gives us the motivations and methods for spreading the gospel. Both Mez and I are convinced Calvinists. We believe that God graciously plans and executes the salvation of people who cannot and will not choose him otherwise. And while some people object that the "doctrines of grace" destroy our motivation for evangelism (because if God elects and saves, why bother spreading the gospel?), we have found that the opposite is true. After all, would you rather try to convince a spiritually dead person to become alive, or to rely on the Lord, who makes his people alive with Christ (Eph. 2:1–10)? It's not for nothing that Paul precedes Romans 10, his great chapter on the spread of the gospel, with Romans 9, his great chapter on the sovereignty of God in salvation. We cannot be clever enough or clear enough or compelling enough to call spiritually dead people to life. But that doesn't mean that we shouldn't preach the gospel. Our proclamation of the gospel is nothing less than the God-appointed means of saving sinners.

Think about it: if you walk into a housing scheme or a gang meeting and share the gospel, would you rather hope that you can convince someone to believe in Jesus, or know that God will infallibly save any and all of his people in that place? When Paul needed encouragement to continue preaching the gospel, the Lord promised him that he had many people in the city of Corinth who were "his people" (Acts 18:9–10). That's the same hope that motivates our ministries; we hope and believe and pray that the God who saves has people in Niddrie and Sterling Park.

Conclusion

Does a commitment to teaching and believing doctrine hinder the spread of the gospel in hard places? Hardly. In fact, our commission to make disciples and teach them to obey the Lord Jesus cannot be accomplished without such a commitment. It's not enough to demonstrate the love of Jesus to a community in need. It's not enough to work hard to see social structures renewed and repaired. We must speak the actual truths of the gospel, or we only bring glory to ourselves and leave them in their sin and guilt.

Part 2

THE CHURCH
IN HARD PLACES

4

The Parachurch Problem

Years ago I (Mez) was in Cape Town, South Africa, visiting a young man named Andy. Andy was involved in ministry with a parachurch organization that specialized in working among street gangs.[1] He had previously interned for me in Niddrie and had asked me to visit him in the field in order to provide spiritual accountability for him. We went out one evening for a meal with some of his twenty-something friends and coworkers. They were all young, fresh-faced, go-getters who were in South Africa to work for the Lord among the poor and needy.

But as I listened to the conversation among these young missionaries, I was surprised by their utter disdain for the institution of the local church. When I asked them where they worshipped, the answer was sadly all too familiar: "We worship together as friends. After all, where two or three are gathered, Jesus is with us." This was closely followed by, "The local churches aren't doing their jobs, so we will take the church to

---

[1] For the purposes of clarity, let me define my use of the word *parachurch*. As I understand it, a parachurch organization normally is a formalized group that engages in social welfare and evangelism without connecting its work to a specific church or group of churches. The stated aim of many of these organizations is to work alongside churches to assist them in doing some specific aspect of their work.

the people." Warming to their theme, one young lady proudly informed me that she didn't need to be in a local church to prove her love to Jesus. (Sadly, she later returned home and no longer worships Jesus anywhere.)

What these young people had done, in effect, was swap the local church family for the Christian ministry they worked for. In this new family everybody looked like them, talked like them, thought like them, and cherished and fought for the same passions as them (the poor, the needy, and gang members in this case). This suited and played into their "us against the world" mentality.

But this is spiritually dangerous. Here they were, all the way out in South Africa with little spiritual accountability except the manager assigned to them by their organization. They were the only Christians around, a group of spiritually immature friends who were likely to support unquestioningly each other's views on life, God, and the local church. When I pointed out to one young lady that her ministry seemed to lack an understanding of the importance of the local church, everyone sneered. Here's the line I will never forget: "Poor people need Jesus more than they need the local church." Her friends congratulated her on a line well said, and the conversation moved on, which was good as I was getting ready to smack everybody in the room.

I was stunned: here were living, breathing, functioning parts and organs of the wider body of Christ, unprepared and unwilling to contribute to the life of a local body! They just didn't see the problem that Paul was so clear about in 1 Corinthians 12:18–21: "But as it is, God arranged the members in the body, each one of them, as he chose. If all were a single member, where would the body be? As it is, there are many parts, yet one body. The eye cannot say to the hand, 'I have no need of you,' nor again the head to the feet, 'I have no need of you.'" These young limbs were wandering around without a body, and they didn't see the harm or danger in doing so.

I reflected further on all this on my flight home. Were these young people entirely at fault for their attitudes toward the local church? Was it just bad teaching and discipleship at a local church level? Did the problem lie with the parachurch organization that employed them? I felt sure that the answer included a number of factors. However, misguided though some of these young people were, they weren't all bad, and, for some, their motives were God honoring. Andy was a prime example. He says this about his time there: "When planning to go to South Africa, my mind was set on being as radical as I could be. I went out with a friend to change a whole township for Jesus." This was a godly, conscientious young man. He wasn't looking for fame and fortune. He just wanted to serve his Lord and Savior among the poor. But rather than see the local church as a vehicle for his ambitions, he recalls thinking about it as "a hindrance to what I wanted to do."

He regarded the Christian agencies that he served with as a solid alternative to the local church. After all, he had read the stories of great men of faith like C. T. Studd and Hudson Taylor who had done great things for the nations without much need for the local church. He had decided that he could serve God more effectively among the poor in a specialized Christian organization that appeared better equipped to do the task than a church, which he described as nothing more than a "boring, structured set of meetings."

The Problem with the Church Is the Appeal of the Parachurch

Andy and his friends are not the only Christian workers I've met who have little use for the local church. Several years after my trip to South Africa I tried to pull together a meeting of pastors and church leaders who were ministering in housing schemes around Scotland. I sent out invitations to various churches and put the word out on the evangelical grapevine. A friend even agreed to let us use his house in the country-side for a couple days. While several people attended, only one was a pastor. Indeed, even that gentleman was more of a missionary trying to establish a work in a scheme (over many years), with little evidence of conversions. All of the others worked for Christian organizations, and most were youth and children's workers.

As the meeting progressed, what I had hoped would be an exchange of ideas and resources turned into a protracted counseling session. The youth and children's workers were depressed. They were largely working outside the parameters of local churches, most of which were uninterested in them or incapable of handling the troubled youth and children they worked among. Plus, they were working with little to no ac-countability in their personal, spiritual lives.

As a result, the majority of these Christian workers were overwhelmed by the scale and difficulty of the ministry in which they were engaged. It even came out that one of the youth lead-ers was embroiled in all sorts of sins, including persistent por-nography. By the end of our time, I was pretty sure that he was not even born again. The whole experience left me deflated and fearful for the future of Christianity in Scottish housing schemes. It felt like we were fighting a forest fire with water pistols. What were we going to do?

If church leaders want to have a serious discussion about these kinds of issues, then we need to face up to some hard reali-ties. The fact is that in Scotland and all over the United States right now many of our poor communities lack a solid, living, localized gospel church. The vast majority of churches that do exist on the ground are either dead liberal churches preaching a Christless message or aging orthodox churches with a gospel nobody is listening to. Churches are doing very little when it comes to taking the gospel to the poor and downtrodden parts of their cities and neighborhoods.

And if we are honest, we have to admit that many churches have neither a plan nor the resources to reach out to the poor on their doorstep, even if they do have a heart for them. Few churches know how to effectively evangelize in poor communities, and perhaps even fewer have a plan in place for discipling people who might come to Christ. In addition, the amount of time, effort, manpower, and money required to make a dent in poor areas is so enormous that it seems like a mountain to climb for the average local church that is fighting to keep its head above water. The result is that few churches who attempt to engage in these areas and among this demographic rise above hit-and-miss evangelism or crisis ministries such as food banks. Many therefore shrug their shoulders resignedly and let the specialized parachurch folk get on with the bulk of the work.

Is it any wonder that concerned believers and spiritual entrepreneurs have seen a gap in the market and attempted to fill it with specialized ministries? This is why in schemes and many other poor areas worldwide we find a proliferation of Christian youth organizations, children's organizations, food banks, clothing banks, breakfast clubs, and emergency homeless shelters. And frankly, it is hard to criticize well-meaning brothers and sisters who have stepped into the breach to meet otherwise unmet needs. Unlike these specialized ministries in poor areas, which are often a hive of activity, the churches in these poor places are burying more people than they are baptizing.

Compare that to the work of specialized parachurch organizations, many of which bring in tons of money on the back of great marketing strategies, a full-time fundraising department, a savvy multimedia online presence, and exciting opportunities for young people to serve in some of these difficult areas. There really is no comparison. Andy summed it up perfectly: "Why would I work for a church? It would mean being held back by structure, authority, and being antiradical. When I read the New Testament, I see life and dynamism, not tired, boring traditions. I didn't want to give my life to that."

It's easy to sympathize with those who feel like it's more exciting to talk about "being the church" instead of joining one. We should not blame specialized ministries for coming to the schemes, housing estates, and bad neighborhoods when churches have neglected their duties or just don't exist. Absent healthy churches, we cannot wholly blame our youth who follow these Christian organizations working outside the confines of local churches. Like moths to a flame, they are welcomed with open, often uncritical arms.

Again, why would energetic young world-changers stick to a local church full of aging people hanging on desperately to their irrelevant traditions, when a world of excitement and service awaits them outside these confines? Why should they bother trying to push new ideas, when local church leadership is often closed off and has been run for decades by men who are out of touch with the world and hanging on to power? Who wants to be led by a bunch of fossils who always play it safe and kill anything new stone dead? As Andy recalls: "I was looking for more and thought that a specialised organisation would bypass all that structure and that I could start something different that was going to be more radical and biblical."

This kind of attitude raises a host of questions:

- What do we do when churches are unwilling or unable to connect effectively with poorer communities on their doorstep?

- Do churches actually hold young men and women like Andy and his friends back from getting into the hard places of the world?
- Should anything be done to stop young people like Andy from jumping the local church ship and boarding specialized organizations for doing work in poor communities?
- Are specialized ministries in fact better at caring for the poor and needy? Are they the solution?

The Pitfalls of the Parachurch

My family and I spent five weeks in New York City several years ago. It was a place we had seen on TV, read about in glossy magazines, and dreamed about seeing, never thinking it would become a reality. When we heard we were going, the mere thought of it made Edinburgh seem gray and dull by comparison. We had built the place up in our minds and brimmed with excitement as we waited to get there. Upon arrival, the city did not disappoint. It was huge and vibrant compared to Scotland's capital. It was busy, loud, colorful, and energetic. We loved it, and it surpassed every expectation we had.

But once we'd been there for a few weeks and ridden the world-famous subway, we began to see the New York behind the big, brash facade. While waiting for our train one day, my youngest daughter counted over twenty rats scavenging for food on the rails beneath us. And although Central Park was beautiful, it was full of homeless people and beggars. Beneath the art, architecture, and splendor of the city lay a lot of sin, vice, and suffering. All was not how it appeared. Of course, we weren't naive enough to think of New York as a sinless paradise, but the experience reminded us that everything around us is broken. A lot of things seem good on the surface, but you have to scratch the surface to see what's underneath.

In the same way, the church is an easy target for criticism. Many things might be wrong with the church. But the same can be said of parachurch ministries, particularly when it comes to working in poor communities.

One of the big claims of those supporting parachurch ministries—particularly those that operate within the context of the poor—is that they can effectively do what the church cannot. On one level that is true. Hundreds of thousands of people in Scotland are doubtless grateful for the food parcels they've received as the worldwide credit crunch bites. Yet observing twenty-first-century Scottish schemes with their history of parachurch involvement, one has to wonder, where is the long-term spiritual fruit after decades of parachurch labor? Where are the indigenous converts? Where are the healthy local churches? In my observation, they are nowhere. In fact there are fewer churches in these areas, not more.

That may seem harsh, but we have to face the hard facts. As Carl Trueman once said, "The parachurch exists purely and solely to serve the church in a subordinate and comparatively insignificant way."[2] Maybe this great parachurch experiment has not helped the local church after all. Whisper it softly, but maybe in some areas parachurches have weakened and not advanced the kingdom of God nor built up Christ's bride. So, for example, I have church members who are forced to miss three out of four Sunday services "working" for their parachurch organization. Where are they worshipping in community? Nowhere. They have been taught that loyalty to their organization is the height of worship.

Granted, we hear lots of stories and read lovely newsletters telling of young people who have "made decisions" or been helped in myriad ways, but then what? If we are going to ask

---

[2] "How Parachurch Ministries Go Off the Rails," *9Marks*, March 1, 2011, http://9marks.org/article/journalhow-parachurch-ministries-go-rails/.

hard questions of the church, we have to ask them of the parachurch as well:

- A decade later, where are all of these people who made decisions for Jesus? Of which church are they members? How have they been discipled?
- Where are the indigenous leaders and executives of these organizations who have evangelized, discipled, and grown converts from the ground up?
- Have we considered the downside of evangelism without meaningful connectivity to a local church? What's the point of a cup of water in the desert when it is miles from any constant water source?

Rather than aiding the local church, our fear is that many parachurch ministries are in direct competition with it. For example, a few years ago our church decided to fund a twelve-month church planting survey in a housing scheme. We paid the salary of a young family who moved into the area in order to carry out a detailed feasibility study. We weren't convinced of the need for a plant and so wanted to get a clear picture from somebody on the ground. Shortly after the family moved in, an executive from a national parachurch organization contacted me. She was furious that we hadn't sought their permission to be there and demanded to know why her group had not been informed.

My response was that we were doing a survey of the area and the man on the ground would be in contact, make any necessary observations, compile a report, and submit it to our church elders for discussion and prayer. In the end, it turned out that a church plant was not going to be workable. Instead we decided to support a young couple from another denomination already planting there. But the response of the parachurch agency to the "threat" of our ministry was to hire a full-time community worker for the area to ensure locals stayed faithful to their brand.

Now, understand that this group complained about a lack of a local church in that community. They publicly portrayed themselves as seeking meaningful partnership with a local church. But the reality was that a functioning local church would, in their eyes, harm their ministry (and their funding), and so they did what they could to make sure that we did not interfere with their market share.

So what can we say about the failings of churches with respect to the poor? Well, surely the answer cannot be more parachurch organizations. Despite the glitz and glamour that surround many parachurch ministries, they have not been ordained by God in the same way as the local church. Despite the failings and weaknesses of churches, they remain the one institution on earth established and sanctioned by God for the explicit work of gospel ministry, both in the hard places and elsewhere. We will consider the role of the church in the next chapter.

5

The Local Church Solution

"If we do not prefer the Church to all the other objects of our solicitude, we are unworthy of being accounted among her members."

John Calvin, *Commentary on the Book of Psalms*

Sometimes the world makes you sick. Picachu was about ten years old when I (Mez) met him. Cute as a button and extremely friendly, he was living in a bush under a dirty yellow sheet with a group of about ten other children. He was one of the oldest, and he was fiercely protective of his little *familia*. I had just started a ministry bringing juice and fresh bread onto the streets in an effort to contact the many street gangs of Sao Luis (Brazil), and Picachu and I became firm friends almost immediately.

His face became more familiar, older, and tired over the few years I knew him. I saw him every day. He would hug me fiercely, and then we would sit down to drink and eat, and I would share the hope of Jesus with him and his friends. He listened intently and would often ask me to pray with him.

Sometimes we would sing a couple of choruses together. One day I asked him where he came from, and he told me. When I asked him if he missed his family, he told me that he did. Reluctantly, he agreed to go with me on a visit in an effort to reunite them and hopefully get him off the street and back into school.

After much effort, we finally found the place on the edge of a rubbish dump. The family "home" was made out of wooden crates, old fence posts, bits of car, and dirt. The smell from raw sewage, which ran in rivulets through the middle of the wooden flooring, was overpowering. Eleven people lived in this place that was no bigger than our average bathrooms. It was horrific. Little wonder that Picachu saw the streets as a far better option.

I imagined that the boy would be welcomed home, a little bit like the Prodigal Son. But as soon as his mother saw him, she started shouting obscenities and screamed at me to take him away. At one point she even offered to sell him to me. Later, an old man shuffled out of the house and began hitting the boy without any provocation. We beat a hasty retreat, and later I found out that his mother was telling him to go away and die and that the old man was his grandfather, who had been having sex with him since he was a baby.

I remember walking away from the community, with hundreds of babies and toddlers playing in the streets, and realizing I had stumbled upon the breeding ground for the next generation of Picachus. I felt sick, angry, and hopeless. The occasional piece of bread, cup of juice, and nice Bible story appeared useless in the face of this boy's soul-crushing reality. Something more was needed, and I had to admit that I didn't know what it was.

I did everything I could for children like Picachu in my limited capacity, but the harsh reality was that my ministry on the streets wasn't really making much of a difference in the lives of these young people. The best we could do was crisis intervention; there was no lasting hope or change. Those kids that we placed in care homes would often escape within a few days only to be back on the streets begging and selling themselves for drugs. Far too many youngsters became "regulars" at our drop-in centers. To the outsider we looked busy (because we were), and to First World supporters that meant great photo opportunities and success in terms of ministry. But I lived with the truth every day. Honestly, I felt depressed by the whole merry-go-round of our work.

Things came to a head for me one day in a quite unexpected way. I turned up at Picachu's usual hangout, and found more children than normal there that day. As I approached, I heard the cry of a baby being cradled in the arms of a child no more than twelve or thirteen years old. It turned out she was the baby's mother and had just given birth. When I asked the mother about *her* mother, she told me that this baby's grandmother was herself a street child in her midtwenties in another part of the city. The societal, institutional, and intergenerational nature of this problem hit home.

As I was gathering my thoughts, Picachu approached me beaming from ear to ear and introduced me to his *irma* (sister). She was unbelievably adorable with golden skin and brown, puppy dog eyes. When I asked Picachu what she was doing there with him, he replied, "She has come to live with us, pastor. They all have. They heard about the pastor who feeds us and loves us, and so they have come." His arm swept around to his little band that had now swelled to about twenty children.

I was speechless. My ministry was supposed to be about getting children off the streets and back into their homes, but instead it was unintentionally drawing children onto the streets and away from their families (such as they were) and their communities. I had seen the rat holes and abusive situations from which they had escaped, but I couldn't justify this.

Other friends had dealt with this problem by opening homes for the children. But many of these homes, though doing amazing work, were themselves nothing more than revolving doors as children moved in and out with alarming frequency. I had to reevaluate everything I was doing.

A Local Church Solution

In an effort to get at the source of the street child problem in our city, I began to trace where these children came from. It became apparent that a majority of them came from one particular poor area on the outskirts of the city. So one day I went to that neighborhood with some Brazilian coworkers, and we began to talk about the possibility of starting a church in the middle of this community. Within months we had acquired some land and built a community center, a small school, and a soccer field, and the Good News Church was born.

With a small band of Brazilians, we began to meet for Bible studies and a small Sunday morning service in our new building. Soon locals came, heard the gospel, and were saved. As part of our discipleship process we trained them for work, educated their children, and offered sporting activities and children's clubs.

The difference was amazing. In my two years working with children on the streets, we had not managed to rescue one child from that lifestyle. Despite appalling and dangerous conditions, most of them just didn't want to change their lives, even when we took them home and clothed and fed them. They had grown accustomed to their lifestyle and the freedom it afforded them. However, during my time with the Good News Church (and in the many years since my departure) countless children were prevented from ever falling into that world. All of this was because of a simple change of strategy—from working in crisis prevention to establishing a gospel-preaching church that welcomed the poor and sought to minister to the whole of life. It was slower work. It was more costly financially and personally. But I remain convinced of its merits in the battle for the lives of the street children of Brazil.

Does the Local Church Really Matter?[1]

In a word, yes. Despite everything we have said about the failures of the local church and the relative attractiveness of many parachurch ministries, Mike and I maintain that healthy, gospel-centered local churches are the God-ordained way to do ministry in hard places. Some might think that it doesn't really matter who does the job, so long as Jesus is made known. But we think that the church matters for a number of reasons.

1. The Local Church Is the Way God Intends to Accomplish His Mission in the World

It is primarily through the church that God wants to make himself known. The local church is God's primary evangelism strategy. So, for example, when the apostle Paul reflected on his ministry strategy, he wrote, "From Jerusalem and all the way around to Illyricum I have fulfilled the ministry of the gospel of Christ; and thus I make it my ambition to preach the gospel, not where Christ has already been named, lest I build on someone else's foundation" (Rom. 15:19–20).

Paul thought of the region from Jerusalem to Illyricum (what we would call the Balkans today) as being reached with the gospel. The ministry of the gospel was "fulfilled" there. Was that because Paul had preached the gospel in every community and home in that vast area? Of course not. Instead, Paul could

---

[1] J. Mack Stiles gave a helpful definition of a local church: "The church is the God-ordained local assembly of believers who have committed themselves to each other. They gather regularly, they teach the Word, celebrate communion and baptism, discipline their members, establish a biblical structure of leadership, they pray and give together," "Nine Marks of a Healthy Parachurch Ministry," March 1, 2011, 9Marks, www.9marks.org/journal/nine-marks-healthy -parachurch-ministry.

check this part of the world off his list because *he knew there were churches in these places.* Paul knew that the churches there were how the gospel would spread into all of the individual neighborhoods. Local churches do local evangelism.

The church is right at the heart of God's plans for mission. This is why, when the apostle Paul sent men like Titus and Timothy to encourage believers, he did so in order to build up local congregations, not to establish independent parachurch organizations. In fact, pretty much all of the New Testament epistles were written (and are still applicable) to specific churches. In short, God has chosen the local church, and no other human organization, to be his kingdom representative to the world.

2. The Local Church Should Matter to Us Because It Matters to God

The apostle Paul wrote to the church at Ephesus, saying: "And he put all things under his feet and gave him as head over all things to the church, which is his body, the fullness of him who fills all in all" (Eph. 1:22–23). The church is Jesus's body here on earth. This universal church is made up of all sorts of people from all walks of life: Jews and Greeks, men and women, educated and uneducated, slaves and free. The same is true whether we are in Niddrie or rural America. If we follow Jesus, we are all one in him, whether we live in Washington, DC, or Edinburgh. Together we represent Christ here on earth through our local body of believers. Therefore, the church is central to the purposes of God and is of benefit to the world around us—even today in our increasingly hostile culture.

God has designed the church primarily for his glory. Ephesians 3:10 informs us that it is through the church that God means to make known his manifold wisdom. Regardless of the failings of every church, every true church is a showcase for God's infinite glory and wisdom. The Bible teaches us that the church is central to the very purposes of God. Therefore, it ought be central to the life of every true Christian. Paul says, "Husbands, love your wives, as Christ loved the church and gave himself up for her. . . . For no one ever hated his own flesh, but nourishes and cherishes it, just as Christ does the church" (Eph. 5:25, 29).

Jesus loves the church despite its many shortcomings and seeming irrelevance to the watching world. The church is his bride and he has no plans to take another. In Acts 20:28 we read that Jesus has built the church with his own blood. The church is built for Jesus, by Jesus, and on Jesus. It is simply unthinkable then to separate Jesus from the local church. If the gospel is the diamond in the great salvific plan of God, then the church is the clasp that supports it, holds it up, and shows it in its greatest light for the world to see.

3. The Local Church Is Where the Believer Grows

The local church is also important in the life of every professing Christian since it is here that we learn doctrine, receive reproof, and train in righteousness. Paul reminds the church at Ephesus that Christ himself "gave the apostles, the prophets, the evangelists, the shepherds and teachers, to equip the saints for the work of ministry, for building up the body of Christ, until we all attain to the unity of the faith and of the knowledge of the Son of God, to mature manhood, to the measure of the stature of the fullness of Christ" (Eph. 4:11–13).

In a scheme like Niddrie, people need the concerted time and effort that only a local church can provide. Very often people will turn up on our doorstep having heard the gospel through some parachurch ministry. Yet they almost always have large gaps in their biblical knowledge and Christian behavior. Without a local church committed to patiently teaching and training them, these people will flounder indefinitely.

Ron is a prime example of this problem. He was a young man who came to us after having spent some time with a Christian organization that helped him deal with his addictions. During that time, he had made a profession of faith in Jesus and had been seeking to live as a Christian upon his release from the program. He had a Bible and access to the Internet but little exposure to Christian fellowship within a local church.

As a result, everybody he ever knew who had professed faith was an addict, and his whole Christian experience was formed around addiction. He had never really mixed with anybody outside of this cultural worldview, and he had not grown much beyond "Come to Jesus and try to stay clean." He was a genuine believer, but he was spiritually malnourished in terms of the Word and church community.

Ron was in a dangerous place spiritually, but he still needed to be brought along slowly. He had jumped about from pillar to post, picking up theological and doctrinal scraps from a number of congregations. Because he hadn't been reared on a healthy spiritual diet, he went into extreme shock once we began to feed him even the simplest biblical truths.

We had to slowly feed him basic truth about God's holiness, sin, and biblical repentance. This was rich food for his soul, and he found it difficult to stomach at first. Indeed, he kicked against it and rejected many things we in evangelical churches would take for granted, such as the fact that all people are born under God's just wrath. The organization that had originally helped him with one issue—his addiction—was not equipped to help him grow and become a spiritually well-rounded Christian.

When he came to our church, he met people who were like him (very important) and people who were very unlike him (just as important). What was interesting was observing how he processed the information he received and battled with it in community. Were people really all born sinful? Was the whole world really under the wrath of God outside of Jesus? Were his unbelieving family and friends really going to hell? He needed people around him to help him process such questions. He needed people who had come from tough backgrounds but who had battled through the same issues and come out the other side. He also needed people who had come from more settled backgrounds and fought through different theological problems. He needed to be exposed to the whole counsel of God and rely on that as his ultimate truth, not his feelings. Unbeknownst to Ron, this was all part of the growing experience for him (and for those around him).

After an initial struggle, he was baptized and became a church member. Now he had a network of relationships across social divides. No longer were his friends just like him. No longer did a pool of ignorance surround his life when it came to spiritual matters. More importantly, Ron began to see the importance of the local church. As his Bible knowledge slowly grew, so did his faith. It was a battle for him in the early days but he hung in there (as did we), and today he continues to grow as a Christian as he studies to become a building professional. It was only when Ron rubbed up against other repenting sinners that his own sins came to light, and it was only when he confessed these frustrations and sins to mature brothers that he could understand repentance, sanctification, and perseverance. In short, it was a church that helped bring the Scriptures to bear upon his life. As Ron says now, "It's a pain, but the local church saved my life."

4. The Local Church Is the Place Where Believers Must Submit Themselves to Spiritual Authority

People in the schemes of Scotland have a problem with authority. Any and all authority figures are regarded with suspicion and derision. I see it throughout the culture of the Niddrie scheme, from an almost universal disdain for the police to the way players behave on our local football team. Every week we work with young men, training them for football games.[2] Yet they will not accept criticism or input from anybody they regard as an authority figure.

When these kinds of people come to Christ, this attitude has to be dealt with immediately. God calls Christians to submit to spiritual leadership, and the best and safest place for them to do this is within a functioning local body of believers. The author of Hebrews is clear about this: "Obey your leaders and submit to them, for they are keeping watch over your souls, as those who will have to give an account. Let them do this with joy and not with groaning, for that would be of no advantage to you" (Heb. 13:17).

Elders are called of God to oversee the local assembly of believers: "Pay careful attention to yourselves and to all the flock, in which the Holy Spirit has made you overseers, to care for the church of God, which he obtained with his own blood" (Acts 20:28). All believers, therefore, should be members of a local church and under the care and oversight of the elders. Believers who are not a part of a local church are simply not obeying God. In fact, they are sinning against him. Jonathan Leeman puts it this way: "Christians don't join churches. They submit to them."[3]

A culture that despises any kind of authority needs to see healthy models of leadership and submission. And the best place for people to see this modeled is in the local church.

5. The Local Church Is the Best Place for Spiritual Accountability

Many years ago I spent some time with a parachurch worker. He was known as a bit of a character. His organization was

---

[2] Mike's note: sadly, Mez is talking about soccer here, not real football.
[3] *Church Membership* (Wheaton, IL: Crossway, 2012), 30.

proud of him. He did brilliant work with children who came from difficult backgrounds. They flocked around him, and his picture was often in the organization's glossy brochures.

But personally he was a complete mess. He confessed to me that he hadn't read his Bible for years. He was addicted to online porn sites. He regularly went out drinking with his non-Christian pals. But as long as he was working his hours, doing his children's clubs, and providing photo opportunities for his supporters, then his organization was happy and had little to say to him. Everybody was busy, and there wasn't time for much more than monthly team meetings and yearly appraisals.

Because this man had no serious spiritual accountability, he had been drifting spiritually for years. He wasn't really part of any local church; when he did go to church, he chose a different one each time. That was enough to satisfy people at work, but it allowed him to stay anonymous in the places he visited.

Is this man too extreme an example? Maybe so. But I fear his experience isn't far off the mark for many who work for parachurch ministries. I have met and counseled far too many to be fooled into thinking this man's story is an anomaly.

All Christians need the spiritual accountability and discipline that being a member of a local church brings. It stops us from drifting. It offers a context for encouragement and rebuke. It provides a community to stir one another on to love and good deeds. Some people argue that their parachurch ministry is their community, or that their friends are their community. But accountability is not just a friendly chat with our pals; it's a humble submission to our church leaders and other members.

6. *The Local Church Is the Place from Which Discipline Is Biblically Administered*

There is little point in complaining about the lack of discipline in parachurch organizations. It is not their job. The job of disciplining unruly or openly sinful believers belongs to the local church (Matt. 18:15–17; 1 Cor. 5:1–13; 2 Thess. 3:6; Titus 3:10).

Take Rab as an example. After he was saved out of a drinking background, he joined our church, got baptized, and was going great guns—until one day he decided to run off and get drunk. He decided to join another church that wouldn't hold him accountable. We called him. We spoke to his parents. We prayed for him.

Ultimately, though, we had to put him on the church care list. This meant that we called a members meeting and shared what was going on with the congregation. We announced that we were going to give members one month to write, e-mail, or phone him and encourage him to return to the Lord and to the church. This process doesn't always work, but with Rab it did. Within a week Rab was repentant and back in the church. What a witness to the church and to the watching community!

If you read your Bible, you will see the church all over the place, but you won't see parachurch ministries anywhere. Now, to be clear, both Mike and I think that many parachurch ministries are great. We simply object to parachurch ministries that compete with or replace the local church, whether they mean to or not. Instead, they should see their role as building up and serving the spread of the gospel *through* congregations in their community.

6

The Work of Evangelism

The schemes of Scotland are in trouble. Based on my (Mez) conversations with brothers in the United States, I would say that American trailer parks and inner cities are as well. The churches in these areas are in decline and have been for a number of decades. Much Christian ministry is happening in these areas: soup kitchens, breakfast clubs, and all sorts of youth work. But very little evangelism that is tied to a healthy local church is taking place.

Fifty years ago in Scotland, mission halls were thriving in the housing schemes of our big cities. City-center churches often saw them as places for young preachers to get an opportunity to practice their craft. Unfortunately, these churches never encouraged the young men to stay there and establish local churches. People were converted through the preaching, but these converts were not gathered together into indigenous churches. Instead, the converts moved out of the schemes as quickly as they could.

As a result, the gospel landscape in these places today is

bleak. Health-and-wealth preachers, ill-equipped parachurch organizations, and government social agencies fill the vacuum. The remaining churches that have fought for doctrinal purity at the expense of cultural engagement now find themselves on the fringes with aged, dying congregations. They have a gospel, just nobody to preach it to. Meanwhile, the churches that adapted to and engaged with culture at the expense of biblical truths tend to be socially conscious, but, ironically, they have the same kinds of aged, dying congregations. They are viewed as little more than social work agencies.

Here's what it looks like in practice:

- Jim has attended the little mission hall in his scheme for fifty years. He remembers the days when it was packed to the rafters and the children's ministry had hundreds in attendance. There are only six of them now; everyone else has died or moved away. The church used to knock on doors and hand out tracts and bring in guest preachers. Those days are long gone.

- Ann goes to the local parish church. It doesn't preach the gospel and only a few people still attend, but she loves the church, and the little homilies on Sunday make a nice break in her week. She's never thought to invite her Indian neighbors to church because her vicar says we're all God's children even though we might worship him in different ways.

- Gary is in his late twenties and has a desire to reach the lost. He works for a Christian charity as a case worker for some of their clients. Gary knows a lot of people in the scheme through his clients, and a few of them know he's a Christian, but none of them really know what that means. Gary is allowed to share his faith if people ask, but he's not allowed to proselytize. It's just easier to keep quiet. Anyway, he is being a good witness just by being in his clients' lives, isn't he?

What would happen if you put these three people in a room? Jim might judge Ann and her church for not being concerned with people's eternal destiny. In return, Ann might look at Jim with disgust. How can they believe all that fire-and-brimstone stuff? Gary would probably look down on both of them and wonder why they can't just get along. Yet the sad reality is that all three are trapped in a downward spiral. How can the gospel spread if churches have lost it? How does Christianity thrive when doing good has replaced speaking gospel truth? The legacy of all three of these approaches is that Christianity is declining. We need to rethink the way we go about evangelism.

Biblical Evangelism Defined

There has been an explosion of interest in mercy ministry among evangelicals. Unfortunately, much of it is pulled along by thoughtless theology. It's not uncommon to hear people talk about evangelism in the following ways:

- Preach the gospel at all times; use words if necessary.
- Evangelism is about what we do as much as what we say.
- Our church focuses on loving people, not recruiting them.
- People need to experience God's love, not hear about his wrath.
- We bring a Bible in one hand and bread in the other.

Are those satisfactory ways of thinking about the task of evangelism? If we want people to be saved by the gospel of Jesus Christ, then we need to understand evangelism. Mack Stiles, in his excellent book *Evangelism: How the Whole Church Speaks of Jesus*, defines evangelism as *teaching the gospel with the aim to persuade*.[1] In his simple definition, biblical evangelism involves teaching and persuading.

---

[1] (Wheaton, IL: Crossway, 2014), 26.

1. Evangelism Is Teaching People

When I first heard the gospel of Jesus Christ, there was nothing flashy about the presentation. There were no smoke machines, no background music, and no altar call, just a command to repent in a cold mission hall in the south of England. Faithful witnesses taught me the good news; men and women opened their Bibles and explained it.

The gospel is a message with objective content, and people must understand that content if they are to come to Christ for salvation. People with no gospel need someone to teach the truth; people with a false gospel need someone to correct the false truth. At its very root, evangelism is teaching people the truth about their perilous spiritual condition outside of Jesus and then introducing them to the good news that there is a way out of the peril. Whatever else we do in difficult areas, our primary purpose must be to teach men, women, and children the message of the Bible.

There are no shortcuts or substitutes to teaching the gospel. People like Jim need to know that biblical evangelism isn't just handing out a leaflet and leaving. It takes more than an invitation to Sunday's service. Ann needs to understand that evangelism is more than being nice and sitting on committees. The Scriptures must be opened and explained. Gary needs to know that the poor need Bible teachers more than they need debt counseling. The most popular and effective ministry we have in Niddrie is our "Wednesday Night No Frills Study." We sit down together for a couple of hours and work verse by verse through the Bible.

2. Evangelism Is Persuading People

In Acts 17:2–4 we read:

> And Paul went in, as was his custom, and on three Sabbath
> days he reasoned with them from the Scriptures, explaining

and proving that it was necessary for the Christ to suffer
and to rise from the dead, and saying, "This Jesus, whom
I proclaim to you, is the Christ." And some of them were
persuaded and joined Paul and Silas, as did a great many
of the devout Greeks and not a few of the leading women.

Conversion is a work of God's Spirit from start to finish, but
people still need to be persuaded. In our teaching, we must be
prepared to give an answer to everyone who asks (1 Pet. 3:15).
My first effort at persuasion was in a church graveyard a couple
of weeks after I had been saved. I was trying to persuade a
friend of mine that life was fleeting and that we needed to be
serious about our souls. I didn't know much except that Jesus
died on the cross; I didn't have any clever apologetics or insight-
ful theological arguments. I only knew Christ was real and that
something inside me had changed forever. So I took my friend
to a graveyard out of sheer frustration at my own inadequacy,
took her to the nearest headstone, and told her that if she didn't
repent of her sins she would die, be buried and forgotten, and
then would burn in hell forever. She got on her knees in tears,
and we prayed together.

I am glad to tell you that I have repented of that form of
persuasion. We want to persuade people, not manipulate them
with fear or promises of good things. Invoking fear in evangelism doesn't work in the schemes, anyway. People's lives are
already miserable. Hope of a better life sells well because it is
what people in the schemes want; that's why the health-and-
wealth guys do so well.

Instead we want to persuade people with the open statement of the truth (2 Cor. 4:2) that is confirmed by an attractive
life. We must live in such a way that people are forced to ask
us about our faith. We cannot transform sinners; we can only
teach and persuade them of the truths of the gospel as revealed

in the Bible. The rest depends on prayer and the sovereign, electing grace of God's Holy Spirit.

Evangelism Sits on a Foundation of Election

Evangelism is fuel for the Christian church—it drives church growth and keeps love for God burning. But some suggest that doctrine is the firefighter who douses those flames with water. Bringing doctrine into a conversation about evangelism is like inviting a firefighter to your bonfire. He will put a damper on the occasion!

But in reality, our evangelism always reflects our doctrinal commitments. You cannot separate your evangelistic methods from the things that you believe about God and salvation. If I believe that sinners freely choose God, then I will attempt to persuade them accordingly. If I believe that everyone goes to heaven no matter what they believe, I, again, will engage with people (or not) in a way that depends on this assumption.

Since all evangelism rests on doctrinal foundations, we ought to rest our evangelism on the Bible's understanding of God's sovereign election of sinners for salvation. John Piper defines unconditional election like this: "Unconditional election is God's free choice before creation, not based on foreseen faith, to which traitors he will grant faith and repentance, pardoning them, and adopting them into his everlasting family of joy."[2]

God has elected and is calling a people for himself from every place on earth. Rich people and poor people will be saved through Jesus Christ, and he will keep them safe forever in his family. Far from killing evangelism, this doctrine not only fuels the fire of evangelism, it keeps evangelism burning indefinitely.

The only way the street gangs of Brazil or illegal immigrants in Northern Virginia are going to be evangelized is through the

---

[2] "Five Reasons to Embrace Unconditional Election," desiringGod.org, July 9, 2013, http://www.desiringgod.org/articles/five-reasons-to-embrace-unconditional-election/.

preaching of the gospel of Jesus. There is no earthly way that we can persuade people to follow Jesus; only God can do that kind of work. If God does not sovereignly save sinners, all of these people are going to hell. It is a great comfort to know that the Holy Spirit will do his job by revealing the truth and drawing lost sinners into a relationship with God the Father and keep them safe forever. That beautiful Trinitarian truth is all the fuel we need to stoke the fires of evangelistic preaching.

Honestly, I would never persevere in this kind of work if I didn't believe that God *will* save people. I used to preach at a youth prison on the outskirts of the Amazon jungle. It was a disgusting place. The heat and stench and noise were overwhelming; the boys and young men were hardened killers. And let me be honest: not once in all my visits did anybody give his life to Christ. Not one made a profession of faith in Jesus. It was dispiriting and depressing, but it was not a waste. The words of Paul encourage me:

> For those whom he foreknew he also predestined to be conformed to the image of his Son, in order that he might be the firstborn among many brothers. And those whom he predestined he also called, and those whom he called he also justified, and those whom he justified he also glorified.
>
> What then shall we say to these things? If God is for us, who can be against us? (Rom. 8:29–31)

Just because I didn't see fruit in that prison doesn't mean it wasn't there. It is a comfort to know that God is working out his wonderful purposes and we get to play a part in his grand, cosmic plan. I have no idea who his elect are; it's not my job to know. My job is to preach faithfully and to persevere until the end. He is working in the child prisons of the Amazon and the church halls of Edinburgh. He is working in the trailer parks of America and the slums of India. He has called, he has justified, and he has glorified. We persevere in the knowledge that because God is sovereign, our labors are not in vain.

Evangelism Should Take Place in the Context of the Church

There continues to be a lot of chatter about "missional living" in many evangelical communities today. If this is just another way to describe living with gospel intent in our daily lives, then I am all for it. Living like this will help to make inroads into our inner-city housing schemes. It will show the world what *evangelistic living* looks like.

Missional living is a great alternative to the "attractional model" approach to evangelism that has dominated the evangelical landscape in recent history. Instead of hiding the gospel behind the safety of our buildings, we have the chance to serve our communities in a variety of ways—in local voluntary organizations, in our schools, at the office. Every time a local community service shuts in Niddrie, our church tries to think of ways we can step into the breach to build gospel relationships.

To my mind "missional living" is not merely about moving into poor communities. It's not just helping somebody find a homeless shelter or a drug rehab. Rather, it's about getting personally involved in messy relationships. It's about helping with childcare issues or marriage struggles or helping a new convert walk through the consequences of past sin such as confessing crimes committed. The good news is that you don't have to know everything about life in a scheme or housing project; people who really care can help people. People who are willing to give it all for Jesus are the ones who make the greatest difference. I am convinced that genuine, ordinary, gospel living always leads to gospel opportunities. Then, when the gospel of Christ is clearly proclaimed, the Holy Spirit will lead people to salvation.

The best context for this kind of evangelism is within the life of a healthy gospel-centered local church. The church equips believers, making sure they understand the gospel and have biblical motivations. It is where believers pray for the spread of the gospel, and where they receive, baptize, and disciple new believers.

Historically, the schemes of Scotland were populated by mission halls, which operated as little outreach stations. Churches would send volunteers to help at clubs or to preach now and again, but these halls had no clear ecclesiology. They were led by committees instead of elders and had no real membership or disciplinary procedures. Evangelism was an event to which you would invite your friends or neighbors after knocking on their doors: come hear the visiting speaker!

The battle in the early days at Niddrie Community was to help people view evangelism as a natural way of life and a daily conversation. At first, some people in the church were not pleased. When we stopped handing out tracts, knocking on doors, and singing carols in the street, I was accused by a vocal few of killing evangelism. Yet when I encouraged these same believers to engage with locals, find out what questions they were asking, get involved in their lives, and share their faith naturally, I was treated like some sort of leper. The problem is that evangelism and discipleship require huge amounts of time and effort—more than many believers are prepared to give. It requires us to love people patiently, going over the same material again and again.

Evangelism Should Take Place in Daily Settings

In Niddrie we find that much of our evangelism and discipleship gets done while giving someone a lift home, to the supermarket, or to the post office. It happens during a ten-minute cigarette break outside the café. It happens at the gym. It takes more than an event or a piece of literature; it requires actually engaging with people and getting involved in the mess of their lives.

How much of our Christianity in the West works like this? How many people in our churches even have the time to pursue active relationships with people outside of their busy schedules? I recently attended a meeting in Scotland and was asked why churches aren't more active in housing schemes. My response was that there were a number of reasons, fear probably among them. One person became agitated. "I'm not scared," he blustered. "I work eighty hours a week. I'm just too busy!" Sadly, he seemed proud of this statement.

Evangelism doesn't start with doing something; it starts with who we are and how we live. It should be as natural as breathing. It is about taking the opportunities to teach and persuade people of the truth of the gospel in the ordinary flow and mundane tasks of life. Instead of expecting people to enter into Christian community, we should be going out and engaging in our communities. Our policy at Niddrie Community Church has been to never start something that our community already offers. It makes more sense for Christians to join existing groups to be a witness rather than expecting unbelievers to come to our groups. We have seen far more people come to faith by taking this approach than by hosting our own events.

Use Events for Friendship Not Just Evangelism

This is not to say we don't run attractional events. In Niddrie our church hosts social events that draw several hundred people. We have singing contests, bingo nights, and prize-giving events, but we never use these events to preach. Instead, we use them to firm up friendships and ensure that our building is seen as a community resource as well as a place of worship. We want people to feel at home among us and not like they will get hijacked every time they come onto the place. We do run two main events a year in which we evangelize people: our Christmas Curry & Quiz Night and our Easter Fry (a full English breakfast followed by a short gospel presentation). Both of these events are well attended, almost exclusively by friends established during other events and in the day-to-day run of our lives. Biblical evangelism can work both informally and formally. There is no need to pitch one against the other.

Play the Long Game

The bottom line is that evangelistic ministry in the schemes is a long, sometimes drawn-out process. Take Jack as an example: he had been a drug user and a dealer for over two decades. He cheated on his long-term partner (and their three children) and was notorious on the scheme. He'd first come into contact with the church through his brother. Jack was loud, aggressive, and opposed to almost everything about God and the Bible. He would come to Sunday services stoned, shouting out and questioning everything said from the pulpit. He wouldn't listen and would disrupt practically every meeting. He was a mess, living a lie, and in complete denial about how bad his life was.

We opened up the Bible and taught him the gospel. We answered his questions about faith and life. We sought to persuade him of the truth about his perilous condition before a Holy God. He would sometimes listen and go away chastened. He would sometimes return issuing threats. But we persevered with him. We prayed for him and his family. We took him to appointments and listened to his sad stories. We were honest with him and spoke truth into his life at every opportunity. He met with me almost daily, but he met with others too. He met with older Christians who spent time with him in the day. He went to members' houses for food. He got involved in our community café. We invited him into our lives, and God, by his Spirit, slowly opened Jack's eyes to the truth about the gospel of Jesus. One day, after being missing for months, he walked into our building and declared that he wanted to hand his life over to Christ.

Despite initial skepticism, we began to disciple Jack, and he began to grow. He swapped his old life and his old friends for a new life with new friends. Before long his partner saw a change in him and she came along to the church and was saved. Within six months of his salvation, he was baptized and then married to his childhood sweetheart in front of their three children and his disbelieving family. There is still a long way to go, but he is moving in the right direction.

We are in a marathon. We don't buy people a bicycle and expect them to win the Tour de France a month later. We need to be patient and long-suffering with people. We will have to repeat ourselves time and again. The best place for all this to take place is in a local, persistent community of gospel lovers who live their lives personally and communally with the intention of teaching and persuading others of the truths of the Bible.

7

The Role of Preaching

Let me tell you about a sermon I (Mike) preached one Sunday morning at my church. Every once in a while, a preacher can tell that he has hit a "home run" with his sermon. The introduction is engaging, the textual explanation is compelling, the illustrations are illuminating, and the application puts the weight of the text onto the congregation. The Holy Spirit brings an intense quiet upon the congregation. Such moments make preaching a delight.

But that was most definitely *not* the kind of sermon I preached on this particular Sunday. My sermon felt like a mess. I was in the second half of a series on Jeremiah. To be honest, I had not planned the series well. The passages were really long. The themes were getting repetitive. And I was afraid that the sermons were not helping the congregation understand the structure of the book. About halfway through this particular sermon, I began to experience the opposite of the "hitting a home run" phenomenon. People were fidgeting and coughing. Only the most dedicated were making eye contact. My illustrations seemed lame. The points seemed obvious and not interesting. Instead of a home run, I could feel my fingers lose their grip on the bat as it went spinning into the crowd.

Finally and mercifully, the sermon stumbled to a halt. We sang a final hymn as I dejectedly returned to my seat, and then we dismissed. As people filed past me on their way out of the building, I could see them struggle to find something to say that was kind but also true.

There was one woman lingering behind the crowd, waiting to talk to me. She introduced herself as a single mother from Colombia. Apparently a friend had invited her to church after a night of heavy partying. When I finally asked her what I could do for her, she blurted out, "In the sermon, you talked about following Jesus. I want to do that. Can you tell me more?"

I was stunned. Yes, the gospel had been made clear in the sermon (at least I got that right!), but it had been presented inside a sermon that was far from compelling. But here was this woman convicted of her sin and her need for Jesus!

Obviously, I do not want to make a habit of preaching boring and poorly conceived sermons. But this incident reminded me of the power that resides in the church's weekly sermon. So as we think through the ways that a church can reach poor communities with the gospel, we must remember that all of our strategies and plans cannot replace the faithful preaching of the Bible. In fact, this is the single most important thing we do.

Preach the *Bible*

Church work in needy places can be intimidating. As we have been discussing throughout this book, the challenges to this kind of ministry are numerous and the progress is often slow. While strategies and methods for reaching these communities might look different from one place to the next, Mez and I are convinced that what people in poor areas need most is the Word of God. Individuals in these communities may well have acute needs for drug and alcohol rehabilitation, education, food, and job opportunities, but none of those needs are as pressing as their need for the Bible.

After all, the Bible is God's appointed means for bringing spiritual life to people. From God's speaking a universe into existence, to his call of Abraham, to the "thus says the Lord" of the prophets, it is God's Word that creates, shapes, and gives life to his people. It is not for nothing that Jesus comes as the Word in flesh, God's ultimate communication to his people (Heb. 1:1–2). And through the Bible God reveals what he is like, what he has done, and how we should respond. God's Word is the way that God brings his people to himself (Rom. 10:17).

Admittedly, this might seem like an odd approach. What good is an old book in face of generational poverty, cycles of abuse, drug addiction, and general hopelessness? But consider what the Bible says about the power of God's Word:

- Paul to the Ephesian elders: "And now I commend you to God and to the word of his grace, which is able to build you up and to give you the inheritance among all those who are sanctified" (Acts 20:32).
- Paul to the church in Rome: "For I am not ashamed of the gospel, for it is the power of God for salvation to everyone who believes, to the Jew first and also to the Greek" (Rom. 1:16).
- And again: "How then will they call on him in whom they have not believed? And how are they to believe in him of whom they have never heard? And how are they to hear without someone preaching? . . . So faith comes from hearing, and hearing through the word of Christ" (Rom. 10:14, 17).
- The author of Hebrews declares: "For the word of God is living and active, sharper than any two-edged sword, piercing to the division of soul and of spirit, of joints and

of marrow, and discerning the thoughts and intentions of the heart" (Heb. 4:12).

A lot of churches never attempt ministry among the poor because they feel like it is a fight they are not equipped to win. Others wade in to the battle but wield the wrong weapons. They go in with handouts and social programs, but there is little life change or visible fruit. But the Word of God is a double-edged sword. It is able to pierce any heart. The Bible is where we find the gospel message, the power of God for salvation. If we have the Word of God applied by the Spirit of God, we have all of the resources we need to minister in any community.

Preach the *Whole* Bible

In some ways, what we are saying goes against one popular approach to teaching God's Word to people with little education or biblical literacy. That approach seeks to engage people in the narrative flow of the Bible, using the stories in Scripture to engage the imagination of the listener and reshape their understanding of the story in which they are living. The thinking is that people are naturally captivated by stories, and so the best way to explain the message of the Bible is to tell the smaller stories that make up the larger story of creation, fall, redemption, and consummation. This method is said to be particularly helpful for people who are not used to sitting still and listening to didactic sermons with lots of propositions.

When that approach is done well (as with the Story of God resources produced by Soma Communities in Tacoma, Washington), it can be an effective tool for sharing the gospel and pressing home the need for faith in Christ. When it is done poorly (as it typically is), it edits the Bible's message and therefore obscures the whole gospel and its power. But what this "gospel storying" cannot be (and, in fairness, its most responsible proponents are not suggesting it should be) is a replacement for the message of the entire Bible. God's Word is not less than a story, but it is not merely a story.

God has chosen to reveal himself through different types of literature. The Bible does contain a lot of stories, but there are also laws, sermons, letters, genealogies, poems, proverbs, philosophical reflections, prophecies, and apocalyptic literature. If you are going to do ministry among poor people, you will need to decide whether you think those communities need to know the whole Bible, or just the stories. Do the people in the homeless shelter in my community need the Psalms? Do the immigrant kids at the local high school need the book of Ecclesiastes? Do the inmates in the local prison need to know what is contained in 1 Peter? We know what the apostle Paul's answer would be, because he defended his ministry in Ephesus by saying, "Therefore I testify to you this day that I am innocent of the blood of all, for I did not shrink from declaring to you the whole counsel of God" (Acts 20:26–27).

If you are an educated person, you will need to be careful not to assume that uneducated people are too stupid to understand the Bible. In my experience, a lack of education usually has less to do with intelligence than it does environmental factors, a lack of genuine opportunities, and (poor) personal choices. But the Bible wasn't written to the faculty of Harvard; it was written to "the low and despised in the world" (1 Cor. 1:28). While we obviously have to exercise wisdom about how to teach through the Bible (it is probably better to start out with a Gospel than to start with Leviticus), we need to be committed to teaching the entire message of Scripture (including Leviticus). We should not edit or redact the Bible by teaching only the parts that *we* think will be useful to poor people.

Preach the Whole Bible Well

People promote various models of communicating the Bible. Some advocate engaging the congregation in a dialogue or telling narratives that communicate a point. But I am convinced that the main diet of the church should be God's Word declared by a preacher. We live in a world where authority is distrusted and denigrated, and in such a world what sinful humans need most is not a friendly chat between equals but a declaration of God's truth in monologue.

Certainly there should be opportunities for dialogue and questions and the sharing of perspectives in the overall life of a church. Still, we should recognize that preaching reflects the way that God normally speaks to his people. Moses declared the Law of God to the Israelites. The Old Testament prophets declared, "Thus says the Lord." Jesus came saying, "Truly, truly, I say to you." Peter stood in Solomon's portico and confronted his hearers with God's demands. What you do not see is God asking for a back-and-forth chat with his people. They are called to praise the Lord in response to his Word and to obey his Word, but they don't get to add to his Word or to offer their perspective on his Word, as if that perspective carried any authority.

When a preacher stands up, he speaks with the authority of God insofar as he faithfully exposes, explains, and applies the Bible. This is not because he is himself inerrant and authoritative, but because the Bible is. To the degree that the preacher is declaring God's Word accurately, his words are God's words, and people should close their mouths and listen. He need not be embarrassed of that authority or shrink back from it, since it is the way that God communicates and gives life to his people. Some people may be offended and think that the preacher's unilateral proclamation of God's Word is a sign of arrogance, but it's just the opposite: listening to God takes humility. The

Holy Spirit will speak so that God's people hear his voice in the preaching of his Word (John 18:37).

Look how serious the apostle Paul is when he commissions Timothy to preach God's Word:

> I charge you in the presence of God and of Christ Jesus, who is to judge the living and the dead, and by his appearing and his kingdom: preach the word; be ready in season and out of season; reprove, rebuke, and exhort, with complete patience and teaching. For the time is coming when people will not endure sound teaching, but having itching ears they will accumulate for themselves teachers to suit their own passions, and will turn away from listening to the truth and wander off into myths. (2 Tim. 4:1–4)

Paul charges Timothy "to preach" in light of Christ's imminent return and the eternal destinies of Timothy's hearers. The Greek imperative that Paul uses gives the sense of a herald declaring the will of his sovereign. It is not a suggestion, but a declaration of what God has done. Add to preaching the commands to reprove, rebuke, and exhort, and you have a picture of an activity that isn't aimed at including the thoughts and comments of others.

Preach the Whole Bible *Well*

Now, please do not misunderstand me. Despite the fact that God's Word is powerful and that God can use even a substandard sermon, we should work hard to preach the Bible well, in a way that connects with people's lives and situations. First, that means our preaching should be *sensitive to our context*; you must have a proper sense of your audience. Whether your hearers are rich, poor, middle class, or a mixture of all three, you will need to be aware of what daily life looks like for them.

If your church is full of middle-class people and all your illustrations cater to them, poorer people will feel less welcome. Do your illustrations assume that everyone has access to a computer? That everyone has been to college? That everyone comes from a stable home? That everyone takes a vacation each year? There is nothing wrong with talking about those things, but do so in a way that acknowledges that such things are not universal.

A preacher must know the cultural values of the place where he is ministering. When I had the joy of preaching in Niddrie Community Church one Sunday, I could see that it is a pretty tough place. The congregation there would not have responded well if I had showed up in a suit and tie and spoken like a seventeenth-century Englishman. Likewise, it would have done them no good if I acted like a superemotional American and tried to help them get in touch with their feelings. Instead, they respected plain speech and responded well to blunt challenges.

Second, good preaching is normally *expositional*. That is to say, good preaching takes a passage of the Bible as its subject and then seeks to expose the meaning of the text to its hearers. I will not belabor this point since I have already talked about the importance of teaching the Bible, but it is my belief that it is best to teach the Bible expositionally through all the different genres of Scripture. This approach teaches people to read the Bible for themselves. It also allows the Bible to set the agenda rather than have the teacher decide what topic needs to be covered in a given week. And, honestly, if you have to cross a cultural boundary to work among the poor (like I do when working with Latin Americans in my neighborhood), you probably do not have a comprehensive grasp of what your hearers need in worldly terms. You *do* know they need the Bible, so it is better to simply speak God's Word by teaching the Bible expositionally.

Third, good preaching is *practical*. Expositional preaching should be very different from the stereotypical (though some-times accurate) picture of the dusty, dry lecture on obscure points of doctrine. It is not enough to simply explain what the Bible says; it must be brought to bear on the unique temptations and challenges and false beliefs that plague the congregation. Good preaching aims at life change, and so the preacher has to help bridge the gap between the ancient text and the world of our hearers (to borrow John Stott's word picture[1]). If you are going to teach the Bible in a poor community, you will need to prayer-fully and thoughtfully apply God's Word to people's lives.

What Kind of Church Do You Want to Be?

I am not arguing for an "if you preach it, they will come" ap-proach to ministry. Preaching cannot be the only thing on your agenda. If there are no people, then there is no one to hear you preaching. Expositional preaching alone will not establish a church in a community where there is none. First, you will need men and women who are willing to invest significant time and energy in sharing the gospel and their own lives with the people of the community. After God (hopefully) saves people and calls together a church, then preaching will play an important role in the discipleship of believers and evangelization of the community.

But if you hope to revitalize or plant a church in a poor community, you must recognize the priority of preaching. It is through the declaration of the Word of God that the church will be built. If you are not a preacher, but you want to be part of a team of people doing church work among the poor, then make sure that this is what you are working to see established. As you help direct the shape of the church that is being planted, keep the preaching of the Word of God at the forefront of your expectations. That is the kind of church you want to be.

---

[1] *Between Two Worlds: The Art of Preaching in the Twentieth Century* (Grand Rapids, MI: Eerdmans, 1982), 137.

8

The Importance of Membership and Discipline

My guess is that when you opened this book, you weren't expecting a chapter on church membership and discipline. I (Mike) do not think that I've ever encountered a conference recommending the practices of meaningful church membership and discipline for churches in poor communities. Or have you ever seen a blog post arguing that if your church wants to reach needy people, you need to make a list of members? Probably not.

We have already argued that poor communities need strong local congregations (instead of more parachurch ministries). But here's a crucial bit: both Mez and I are convinced that the practices of meaningful membership and church discipline are vital to a congregation's health and fruitfulness.

Contrary to what its critics might say, the practice of church membership is not an outdated, mid-twentieth-century "business model" approach to church life. Instead, Scripture provides a compelling case that churches should be very clear about who is inside the church and who is outside. In this chapter, I'd like to present that case for church membership and then make a few comments about ways meaningful membership and discipline impact ministry in needy communities.

Insiders and Outsiders

One way to characterize the broad storyline of the Bible is to say that it is the story of God's love for his people and his wrath against his enemies. There is a stark difference between being God's friend and God's enemy. It is not surprising, therefore, that God makes a clear line of distinction between those who are his people and those who are not throughout the Bible—from creation to consummation.

First, in the garden of Eden God's people lived in communion with him. After Adam and Eve's rebellion, he dissolved their immediate fellowship and expelled them from the garden. He established a perimeter around the garden and charged an angelic guard to keep the humans out. While they remained righteous, they were "in"; when they sinned, they were "out."

God then appeared to Abraham in Genesis 12 with a gracious promise to create from his descendants a new people that belonged to the Lord, a new race of "insiders." He reaffirmed this promise in chapter 17: "I will establish my covenant between me and you and your offspring after you throughout their generations for an everlasting covenant, to be God to you and to your offspring after you . . . and I will be their God" (Gen. 17:7–8). This was a promise that a relationship would abide between Abraham's descendants and the Lord that was distinct from the Lord's relationship with all other human beings. There would be two kinds of people: those who are "God's people" and those who are not. An earlier promise to Abraham made the line even starker: "I will bless those who bless you, and him who dishonors you I will curse" (Gen. 12:3).

In order to make this spiritual reality physically apparent, God gave Abraham the sign of circumcision as a rite of initiation and inclusion—an entryway to signify membership among God's people. So significant was this marker that individuals from foreign nations could be included among God's people upon circumcision (Gen. 17:27), and physical descendants of Abraham could be cut off from God's people for refusing circumcision (v. 14). God now provided a clear line of distinction: the circumcised were in; all others were out.

The Levitical law further established and codified this line of distinction. It further served to set the descendants of Abraham off from the rest of the world. God wanted his people to be pure and holy, distinct in everything from their clothes to their food to their worship. Now there was another way to see the distinction between God's people and his enemies: those who kept the law were in; all others were out.

This is why Moses (and later, Joshua) repeatedly told the nation of Israel to remain separate and pure as they took possession of the land of Canaan. Just as they were to live within the *physical* boundaries of the land, they were to live within the *spiritual* boundaries of the Levitical law and holiness code. Joshua warned:

> Be very careful, therefore, to love the LORD your God. For if you turn back and cling to the remnant of these nations remaining among you and make marriages with them, so that you associate with them and they with you, know for certain that the LORD your God will no longer drive out these nations before you, but they shall be a snare and a trap for you, a whip on your sides and thorns in your eyes, until you perish from off this good ground that the LORD your God has given you. (Josh. 23:11–13)

In many ways, the story of Israel is a story of their failure to maintain this distinction. Beginning with the book of Judges, the Old Testament histories chronicle how idolatry and intermarriage made the Israelites indistinguishable from the surrounding nations. Relative to these neighbors, being an Israelite meant less and less. By the time of Israel's exile, only a remnant remained faithful. Since Israel lived and worshipped like a pagan nation, God sent them off to live among the pagan nations. Since the spiritual borders had vanished, he did away with the physical borders of the land. It was no longer clear who was in and who was out.

When we turn to the New Testament, we find that God sent his Son to create a new people for himself, the church. Now both Jews and Gentiles, because of Christ's work, are invited to be God's people through faith. Those who were *once not a people* are *now the people of God* (1 Pet. 2:10). They once were out; now they are in.

Instead of physical circumcision or ethnicity, followers of Christ are identified with the people of God through baptism (Acts 2:41). This baptism symbolizes their identification with the crucified and risen Christ. As Paul wrote: "Do you not know that all of us who have been baptized into Christ Jesus were baptized into his death? We were buried therefore with him by baptism into death, in order that, just as Christ was raised from the dead by the glory of the Father, we too might walk in newness of life" (Rom. 6:3–4).

The coming of Christ and his finished work on the cross created certain discontinuities between the Old Testament and the New Testament people of God. Old Testament Israel was a mixed community, comprised of both physical and spiritual descendants of Abraham (Rom. 9:6–8). Yet the Lord promised through the prophet Jeremiah a new covenant "not like the covenant that I made with their fathers," but a covenant in which "all know me, from the least of them to the greatest" (Jer. 31:31–34). The body of Christ is intended to be comprised exclusively of those who, by faith, have been united to him. In the words of the prophecy, they *all* know the Lord.

This element of discontinuity from the Old Testament to the New Testament will become significant when we consider exactly who is in and who is out among the New Testament people of God. But we should observe the continuity between the people of God in both Testaments: God *continues* to make a distinction between those on the inside and those on the outside. There are those who have been baptized into Jesus, and there is everyone else. Jesus even compared the church to a sheep pen of which he is the door (John 10:7). And a sheep pen has a fence. Jesus also said that he knows his sheep and that his sheep know him (v. 14).

This pattern of inclusion and exclusion will be brought to a head at the consummation of history. At the end of time, God will make a final and clear separation. All mankind will clearly see on that solemn day who dwells among God's people and who does not. The sheep will be separated from the goats (Matt. 25:31–33). Those whose names are found written in the Lamb's Book of Life will be ushered into glory, while those whose names are not written in his book will be cast out (Rev. 21:27).

Membership in the New Testament Church

When we look carefully at the data in the New Testament, it is clear that the early Christian church did practice meaningful membership. While none of these passages are overwhelming on their own, taken as a whole they form a substantial argument. Let's look at five places in the New Testament that point toward the practice of church membership in the early church.

1. Those Reluctant "to Join" the Church

In Acts 5:12–13 we are told, "Now many signs and wonders were regularly done among the people by the hands of the apostles. And they were all together in Solomon's Portico. None of the rest dared join them, but the people held them in high esteem."

Fear gripped both believers in the church and the nonbelievers who heard of the circumstances surrounding the deaths of Ananias and Sapphira.

The anxiety was such that many did not dare "to join" the church, presumably for fear that they would suffer a similar fate.

The Greek word translated as "join" means "to bind closely," "to join together," and "unite." This same word occurs in 1 Corinthians 6:17 to refer to the union that occurs between a believer and Christ. At the very least, the use of the word "join" in Acts 5:13 refers to more than casually *showing up*, as you or I might speak of "joining the dinner party for dessert." The word indicates the existence of some sort of formal connection, more like joining a club.

2. The List of Widows

In 1 Timothy 5:9–12, Paul gives Timothy a set of instructions for enrolling widows on the list of those receiving support from the church. He writes: "Let a widow be enrolled if she is not less than sixty years of age, having been the wife of one husband, and having a reputation for good works. . . . But refuse to enroll younger widows. . . ."

The verb translated "enroll" can be either specific ("to put on a list") or general ("to consider as part of a certain group"). The former meaning would clearly show that the church was keeping an accessible list of widowed members. Yet even the latter meaning would mean that the church was distinguishing between people in a way consistent with the practice of church membership.

Why mention the widow's list? It's difficult to imagine the church keeping a list of widows but not keeping a list of members. If it didn't keep the latter list, what group of widows would even be considered for inclusion on the former list? Any widow in the entire city of Ephesus? The widow who showed up a few times years ago? Of course not; the church would have some specified pool that it was drawing from.

3. The Punishment of the Majority

In 2 Corinthians 2:6, Paul refers to the discipline the church inflicted on an individual as the "punishment by the majority." We will consider church discipline more in just a moment, but for now it's worth observing that the existence of a "majority" means that there was a defined set of people from which the majority is constituted. There cannot be a majority of an unspecified group; it must be a majority of *something*.

Was it the majority of people who happened to be present the day the vote was cast? Could non-Christians then vote? Could any Christians who happened to be visiting from another city who didn't know the situation vote? The most natural assumption to make is that Paul meant the majority of an acknowledged membership of the church.

4. Accountability to Leaders

The New Testament warns church leaders to discharge their responsibility for oversight diligently. In Acts 20:28, Paul instructs the Ephesian elders to "pay careful attention to yourselves, and to *all the flock*." In Hebrews 13:17, the church is told to respect elders since "they are keeping watch over your souls, as those who will have to give an account."

Who constitutes the flock over which the elders watch? For whom must the leaders of the church give account? The citizens of their city? Anyone who ever attends their church? Of course not. They must be accountable for the members of the church, those whom everyone recognizes as committed to the leaders' care. Church leaders cannot function properly without church membership.

5. Metaphors for the Church

The New Testament uses several metaphors to describe the local congregation. We've seen in Acts 20:28 that the church is referred to as a flock. In 1 Corinthians 12:12 it is compared to a body. In 1 Peter 2:5 the church is pictured as a building.

Each of these metaphors demonstrates an obvious relationship between the individual and the congregation as a whole. The individual Christian is a member of the body and a sheep in the flock. The individual believer is, in Peter's words, "a living stone" in the spiritual house.

Each of these word pictures, so vital to our understanding of the church, demand more than a casual commitment from the individual. There are no informally connected stones in a building. They are cemented together unambiguously. Sheep do not hop from flock to flock; rather, the shepherd knows exactly how many sheep he has in his care. Body parts do not relate to each other informally; they are intricately connected to each other and are mutually dependent. Surely, we best reflect these metaphors when we formally tie ourselves to a local congregation.

Among other pieces of evidence, these five examples suggest that participation in the life of the church body wasn't casual or easily dissolved. It was a relationship that one entered into (joined) and that came with responsibilities (determining discipline, submitting to leadership) and privileges (support for the widows, inclusion in the people of God). It is hard to imagine how this was accomplished without a clear sense of the membership of the church.

Why Poor Communities Need Church Membership

Hopefully you are convinced that the Bible's description of church life requires a clear and established understanding of who belongs in the congregation. I want to take the argument a step further, though: membership is not only biblically required (which, if you are a Christian, is a sufficient reason to do anything), but it is also helpful in creating the kind of healthy congregations that are able to reach poor communities (see chap. 5).

1. Membership Prevents "Second-Class Syndrome"

A subtle caste system can easily develop in a church. People with money or education may be tempted to look down upon and marginalize poorer believers (cf. James 2:1–6). If a church hopes to see people from needy places come to Christ, then they must be sure that those people are welcomed into a full place in the life of the congregation.

Meaningful membership has a wonderful "flattening effect" on the church. Church membership makes is clear that all Christians have the same status together before God; we are simply members of the body of Christ. A congregation that wants to reach out to a poor community must understand this biblical truth. When people come to Christ from needy communities, they should be baptized and brought into the membership of the church. That makes it clear that they are fully accepted and fully functioning parts of the body.

2. Membership Increases Accountability and Connection

Establishing church membership increases the accountability among the congregation and between the congregation and its leadership. Membership requires commitment, and it clarifies in biblical terms what it means to be a part of the church. When people become members of the congregation, they are promising to love and care and pray for and be accountable to all of the other people in the church. This means that all members of the church—rich, poor, and middle class—will be called upon to love each other. In our congregation, we do not only want homeless people and recent immigrants to come to Christ; we also want them to become fully functioning, integrated members of the church.

3. Membership (Including Discipline) Makes It Clear That Someone Is a Believer

In 1 Corinthians 5, Paul instructs the church on how to deal with a man living in open and scandalous sin. For the health of the church, the congregation is told to exercise church discipline against the man by "delivering the man to Satan." In verse 2, he tells them that rather than letting the man remain among them, they should "let him who has done this be removed from among you." There are a few things for us to notice from this passage.

First, the punishment is described in verse 2 as removing this man "from among you." The result of the church discipline is the removal of the sinner from the congregation. This necessarily implies the presence of a formal membership. How else could someone be removed if they did not belong in a formal sense in the first place? Let me illustrate my point. I cannot be removed from the Northern California Left Handed Golfer's Association because I have never been a member of such an organization. Now according to their website, the NCLHGA *will* remove people from membership for several reasons (like right-handedness, perhaps?). But I am in no danger of being subject to such an action, because you can't kick a person out who was never a member to begin with.

Second, the church's discipline is to occur when "you are assembled [together]" (v. 4). For our purposes, simply note that there was a definite and formal assembly of the church, and they knew who was expected to be there when the congregation gathered. Again, this clearly implies meaningful church membership.

Third, Paul means for the church to discipline only those "inside" the church (v. 12). The apostle is not telling the church to police the world and its morality. Obviously, the church knew who was an insider and who was an outsider. Proper church discipline is impossible without defined church membership.

Fourth, church discipline is for the good of the church but also the benefit of the person being disciplined (v. 5). Paul insists that the church put the immoral person outside the membership of the congregation so that his soul might ultimately be saved. We might think of church discipline as something distasteful and harsh, but the apostle clearly thought that it was an act of love toward the sinner. When a person is in good standing in a congregation, he or she possesses some assurance of salvation; an external authority has examined his or her profession of faith and given the thumbs up.

But when a church removes that affirmation through church discipline, the action works as a wake-up call to the person living in sin. His or her profession of faith is called into question by the refusal to repent of sin, and the person in question must face the reality that his or her soul is in danger. Obviously, not everyone who is put outside the church eventually repents and returns. But sometimes by God's grace they do, as in Rab's story back in chapter 5.

Fifth, church discipline shows the world what a Christian should look like. The immorality of the man in Corinth was of the kind that would scandalize even the pagans in the community (v. 1). If the church did nothing, the watching world would be left to conclude that Christians were the worst kind of perverts. But by putting the man outside the church, the congregation made it clear to the world that sin has consequences and that unrepentant immoral people are not truly Christians.

4. A Church's Evangelistic Outreach Depends on Its Distinctiveness

Christians these days often think our evangelistic power depends on showing the world how much we're like them. Yet the challenge for churches today is the same as it's been at least since ancient Israel was tempted to pursue the gods of the nations—being distinct. What good is salt that loses its saltiness? You might as well throw it out. Or what good is a light under a bowl? It's our distinct lives that give the world something for which to praise God (Matt. 5:13–16; see also 1 Pet. 2:9–12).

Healthy practices of membership and discipline play a crucial role in cultivating and protecting the distinctiveness of a church. They are not the primary *cause* of these changed lives. The preached Word is. But the practices of membership and discipline protect those lives, clarify them, and put them on display. How hope-giving do you think it is in a tough community for people to witness an outpost of Christ's kingdom? For locals to see a group of supernaturally changed and changing people?

On the other hand, how much damage to the church's evangelistic witness in the West has occurred because so many church members live just like the world (1 Corinthians 5)—and neither their church leaders nor congregations confront them about it?

Rubber, Meet Road

Working with needy people means stepping into lives that are often messy. Of course, people who are not poor also have messy lives, but poverty exacerbates problems and often flows out of a range of sins that make life very complicated. This means that church membership will bring about some complicated situations:

- Can someone who is in the country illegally be a member? How much should the church ask about a person's immigration status in the membership process?
- Can someone on prescription methadone be a member?
- What if someone comes to Christ after two decades of living with the same person? How quickly must they get married? What if there are children involved? What if each of them is married to someone else back in their home country, but they haven't talked to their spouses in decades?

We cannot wait for people to completely clean up their lives before admitting them to church membership, but we need to be able to affirm credible professions of repentance and faith. A man living with his girlfriend will need to move out. A drug dealer will need to give up his trade. But we don't require perfection of people joining our churches. We do require them to take up the fight against sin—to repent.

In order to sort through these kinds of issues, the elders of our churches interview candidates for membership, explain our statement of faith, talk about their responsibilities as members and ours as leaders, and ensure that they have a clear understanding of the gospel and what it means to live a life of godly obedience. We provide the candidate's testimony to the congregation a week or two in advance of our congregational meetings, and we encourage church members to come forward with any concerns or questions about the person.

Elements of this process are prudential. But our goal in these procedures is to shepherd everyone who joins the church (1) to see the seriousness of claiming to follow Jesus; (2) to understand the importance of the church family; (3) to submit to godly leadership and accountability; and (4) to see the difference between the church and the world and to know for whom they are responsible as fellow members.

But keeping the line clear between the church and world helps not only those inside the church, but those outside. Mez's church once had a man in attendance who claimed to be a Christian, but was dealing drugs, selling pornographic films, and engaging in sexual relations with men and women in the community. People on the street would talk to Mez about this man, allowing Mez both to affirm his care and love for the man, while also explaining that this man only attended the church but was not a member. Good discussions with these "concerned citizens" followed. Mez could explain *why* this man was not a member and what membership meant. In short, keeping the lines of membership clear allowed Niddrie Community to open its doors to this man, but not to vouch for his faith and tell the world he belonged to Jesus. A clear view of membership, in short, helped to ensure that the church's witness in the community was not tarnished by a mere attender, while also demonstrating its love for a man like this.

Acts of church discipline do all this as well. One church intern got a local woman pregnant, which led to much gossip in the community. The church's act of discipline against this man amazed the community—for good! Another act of excommunication led to most of the people in the person's family being evangelized. And they applauded the strong stand of the church, bolstering our credibility in their eyes.

Conclusion

Church membership might seem like a luxury that missional churches cannot afford. Perhaps it provokes images of stuffy, fastidious congregations more interested in cultivating their own little gardens than in taking the gospel into the world. And maybe some churches have fallen into this error. But don't throw the baby out with the bathwater. You cannot blur the line between the church and the world or partner light with darkness (see 2 Cor. 6:14–7:1). Poor communities don't need just another "community center" which hosts various "help the neighborhood" projects and workshops on being responsible parents. They need outposts of Christ's kingdom that are distinct like salt and bright like lights on a hill.

Part 3

THE WORK IN
HARD PLACES

9

Prepare Yourself

Pastors, seminary students, and prospective church planters ask me (Mez) many of the same questions about my ministry in Niddrie. How can we reach a poor neighborhood near our existing congregation? Should we plant a new church or try to revitalise an existing work? How do I know if I am cut out for this kind of ministry? Should we move into a poor area or not?

We don't have time to answer every question in this chapter, but here are some of the more important lessons I have learned along the way.

1. Recognize the Harsh Reality

Just before I arrived in Niddrie in 2007, somebody sent me a copy of *The Scotsman*, a national newspaper that ran the following headline about the church I was going to pastor: "New Church Forced into Fortress Mentality after Vandals Attack." The article began:

A church built entirely on donations from a New Town congregation has been forced to spend £10,000 on "fortifications" after being besieged by vandals who have caused damage running into thousands of pounds. Members of the Charlotte Baptist Chapel in Rose Street pledged more than £700,000 so a new community church could be built in Niddrie. But within weeks of the new church and community hall being completed, it had been repeatedly vandalised, leaving its windows and central heating pipes smashed.[1]

I'd just arrived from working with street gangs in Brazil, so I wasn't completely unaware of the harsh realities of inner-city ministry. But Scotland is very different from Brazil. Despite the violence and poverty, South Americans still had a fear of God and a respect for the church. When I arrived in Niddrie, it became immediately clear that while people might pay lip service to God, they had no respect for this church and even less interest in my ministerial credentials.

I inherited a church building under constant siege by local children and youth. Our windows were often smashed, cars were set alight, and members were assaulted in the street. What made it worse was that this abuse had been going on for so many years that trashing the building was practically an intergenerational rite of passage for local youth. The Christians inside the building, most of whom lived outside the community and commuted in, were easy targets.

The small group of believers I inherited were well-meaning and conscientious, and had a real love for Niddrie. The problem was that they were attempting to arrest decades of decline as cultural outsiders to the scheme. Their only contact with the community was Sunday services and the odd leafleting campaign or door-knocking initiative. Even the way the church services were ordered and conducted seemed calibrated to the

---

[1] *The Scotsman* online, March 18, 2006, http://www.scotsman.com/news/new-church-forced-into-fortress-mentality-after-vandals-attack-1-974347/.

culture of a professional class city-center church, not a church in a poor community.

When the church was looking for a pastor, they wanted a man to come along and continue doing what they had always done. Needless to say, the early months were particularly difficult for me. The church members were preoccupied with the programs. One day I received an e-mail from a disgruntled member who berated me for removing the forty-seven different kinds of evangelistic tracts from the café area (actually, it was the second e-mail of this kind). Apparently I was killing evangelism. Almost simultaneously, another e-mail arrived in which the sender wanted to know why I wouldn't be encouraging the church's choir to walk the streets at Christmas singing carols. Still another member wanted to know whether I'd be doing drama from the pulpit because, if so, he was leaving.

The Niddrie community around us, on the other hand, had a completely different set of concerns. The day before these e-mails came, I spent a few hours with a young man who had been raped as a boy by his uncles and was now selling himself for sex in the town to pay for his crack habit. Another woman had her electricity cut off for nonpayment. In the night some local children had stolen all the drainpipes from the church and smashed up the front steps with golf clubs.

In short, there was a complete disconnect between the people who met in the building and the lives outside.

As I sat there on that cold winter morning by myself, I wondered if and how I was going to be able to turn the church around. When I'd planted a church in Brazil, I had done it from the ground up. So it was easy to infuse gospel DNA into the church. This was a whole different ball game. How was I going to bring these two worlds together? Honestly, I felt like walking out at that moment. In the end I stayed and embraced the fact that it was going to be hard. Churches that exist in poor areas are dying for a number of reasons, and all of those reasons are hard. Planting and revitalizing both are hard work. There is nothing remotely romantic about this work at all.

2. Understand Your Motivation

Visitors often come to Niddrie Community Church, are moved by the ministry, and then say something like, "I have a real heart for this work. I'd love to come back and minister." Without fail I will encourage these people to think about their motivation. Just having an emotional attachment to the work is not enough. Of course these people love Jesus. Yet within weeks of returning home the feelings often disappear, and they return to normal life. The Bible warns us that religious people sometimes have messed up motivations (Matt. 6:1–6; Mark 9:34; 12:38–40).

We had the same issue in Brazil. Workers would arrive and be gone within months, burned out by the overwhelming intensity of the ministry. What looks glamorous in a moving presentation in a mission hall, or what sounds fascinating on the pages of a book, is a bit of a letdown in real life. Beginning a ministry on the strength of personal feelings or some romantic idea of love for the poor is inviting disaster into your life. Having a heart for people and loving the downtrodden is necessary, yes, but it's not enough to get you through the hardships of daily living on the ground.

What is a good motivation for this kind of work? I confess that a smelly and deceitful drug addict does not inspire me to lay down my life for him. Only my love for Jesus allows me to love those rats. Only a true understanding of the grace of God in Jesus and the fact that Christ died for a rat like me, plus a full appreciation of the gospel, allows me to serve people like this cheerfully, despite their indifference and hostility to my help. In the end, I'm not doing it to please them but in loving service of a Savior who has redeemed *me* from the same pit.

One psychiatrist has written,

> As with persons in any other helping profession, sometimes the motivation to enter the ministry is to gain the appreciation, attention, and acceptance which is personally needed but which is not being supplied elsewhere. Sometimes it is the unconscious desire to dominate others and in effect to become little popes, which is an easy goal to achieve if one ministers to immature people. Many pastors receive much unconscious gratification from being able to direct people and set them straight.[2]

I think he is exactly right.

So you should ask yourself: why do you want to minister among the poor? What's your motivation? Social justice and mercy ministries are big news in the evangelical world right now. The reality, as we have already seen, can be somewhat different than the romantic notion many people hold about this kind of ministry. We must be aware of our motivations because they can come back to haunt us if we don't think deeply before we engage in any kind of ministry.

3. Background Isn't the Most Important Thing

Many young men and women have great interest in the ministry of 20Schemes. Most of them come from stable families and are well-educated. And almost everyone's first question is: am I too posh to work in the schemes? It is a good question. Despite objections (usually from those in power) that the issue of class is overplayed, there is a definite cultural divide along class lines

---

[2] Basil Jackson, "Psychology, Psychiatry, and the Pastor: Part II: Maturity in the Pastor and Parishioner," *Bibliotheca Sacra* 135 (April 1975): 111–12.

in the United Kingdom. People feel it and sense it and show it in the ways they walk and talk and dress.

Now, the young people in question wouldn't normally think of themselves as posh. They think of themselves as normal. But they worry that lower/working-class folks will make a class distinction. After all, we "urban poor" don't just have a chip on our shoulders; we have the whole block of wood! To us, "posh" means that you like hummus, both your parents are together, and you probably play board games in the evenings. We like our takeouts and reality TV shows. Posh folk like ballroom dancing, theater trips, and a glass of red wine with friends.

Usually my response to their question is: "Do you think people are going to hell unless they turn from their sins and put their faith and trust in Christ alone for forgiveness?" If they answer in the affirmative, we are in business. If they go red and quibble and generally look uncomfortable, it's probably a good bet that they're not going to be cut out for ministry in our setting. In the schemes, we just want to know that you will give us straight answers to our direct questions.

Of course, class matters at one level. My assistant pastor watches period dramas despite all attempts to rehabilitate him. He even carries a satchel through the streets of Niddrie, and I often have to endure the scorn and shame by walking next to him when he does it. But you know something? Niddrie wouldn't be the same without him. My life wouldn't be as rich. Who would there be to mock his posh ways? In all seriousness, he is known and loved around our scheme, largely because he is a genuine man who loves people and is willing to speak "straight up" into their lives.

My next questions for prospective workers are: Do you know and love Jesus Christ? Do you love people enough to tell them about their sinful condition? Do you love the local church? Are you willing to get deeply involved in messy lives for the long haul? If you are, then the other things just don't matter in the end. There's no need to ditch your man bags and your special edition *Royal Wedding* box set (kept in a drawer, obviously).

Of course, scheme life is a bit of a shock for those not used to it. It's hard to adjust to the mind-set, but it's not impossible. Paul was a Jew of Jews, and he took the gospel to the Gentiles and had to get over a mess of cultural issues to do it. What does it really matter if people bringing the gospel to the poor are sipping chai-tea lattes? People are dying without Christ; that's the bottom line. At the end of the day, it is being a person of real substance who loves Jesus and loves people that truly matters. It might take you longer to fit in, but perseverance, being yourself, and being teachable go a long way to acceptance.

4. Your Family Needs to Be on Board

Inner-city ministry can be a tiring, frustrating, depressing, slow, repetitive, bitter, thankless grind. You may be the object of constant slander and gossip. As a result, your home life is an important ingredient for a healthy gospel ministry. Without my wife by my side, supporting me, praying for me, keeping me straight, and loving me, I don't think I would have lasted this long in the kind of ministry we are doing.

Ministry in a poor community affects my family. I bring random strangers home at all hours for meals, showers, and clothes, often at a few minutes' notice. My wife never blinks. She has a God-given gift of hospitality and an endless patience even with the most garrulous guests. We have sat up nights with people going "cold turkey" on their addictions. We have strangers turn up on Christmas Day for lunch. We have had guests come with us on a family vacation. Yet through it all, we have managed to maintain our love for one another and a deep appreciation of our distinctive roles within the ministry we have.

My home, though often busy, is a calm oasis in stormy times. My wife is not fighting against the ministry and me. We have date nights. We have family nights. We pray together. But when emergencies or a flurry of pastoral issues come, she doesn't add to my pressure by complaining and vying for my attention.

This kind of ministry is immersive. If you like to divide your life into "ministry time," "leisure time," and "me time," then this may not be the kind of ministry for you. You don't have to be married to thrive in our ministry, but if you are then you must have a secure and happy marriage and an immensely supportive spouse. If not, get out quick. I have survived for so long because God is good and my wife makes sure that our home is a refuge from the storms of ministry, even if I sometimes bring a little bit of driftwood home.

5. Your Church Leaders Must Be on Board

From time to time people will turn up at the church having heard about our ministry and us. Usually they are looking to leave their own congregation and join ours because they're interested in ministering among the poor (sometimes they just want to join our church). Without exception, I will ask them about the church from which they have come. Who is your pastor? Does it have elders? What do they say about your plans?

Oftentimes, these kinds of questions are met with confusion. The general attitude is, "What does it have to do with them? I can do what I like." Or, "They don't understand me. God has spoken to me about such and such and they just don't get it." The assumption is that I will understand their vision for work among the poor more than the elders of their church. They could not be more wrong.

The author to the Hebrews reminds us, "Obey your leaders and submit to them, for they are keeping watch over your souls, as those who will have to give an account. Let them do this with joy and not with groaning, for that would be of no advantage to you" (13:17). People are free to feel called all they want, but they need to have that calling validated by those who have spiritual oversight over them.

One thing is for sure: if you cannot submit to your own spiritual leaders, then you should not enter into a ministry where you expect people to submit to your leadership. If your elders and church leaders are not behind you, it is a pretty safe bet that you are not cut out for ministry at this stage. If you are considering church work among the poor, speak to the elders or leaders of your church, and ask them to pray with and advise you.

6. You Need to Pray

When I began my ministry in Sao Luis, nobody else in the city was doing anything to reach the street children. I began praying for a team and the opportunity to reach out to the children. Within weeks I had met an older lady called Otacelia and had begun to gather a small team of interested Brazilians around me. Before we started anything, we agreed to meet daily to study the Bible and to pray together. Every morning and every night we had a prayer meeting before we left for the streets. We continued this practice throughout my time in Brazil.

When I first came to Niddrie Community, I opened the building early in the mornings and began praying for the congregation and the area. As I became more familiar with the place and learned the names of some locals, I began to pray for them too. As people were saved, I prayed for their families. I prayed for more team members. And then something happened: God answered my prayers. This prayer time, begun more than seven years ago, continues almost daily.

Prayer is the absolute key *before*, *during*, and *after* any ministry. After all, we are in a spiritual war. Paul reminds the

Corinthians that "the god of this world has blinded the minds of the unbelievers, to keep them from seeing the light of the gospel of the glory of Christ, who is the image of God." (2 Cor. 4:4). Our Enemy isn't going down lightly. He will use every trick at his disposal to hinder the work of gospel ministry. He will attack your family, friends, church, and neighbors. The Devil, the world, and the flesh are our bitterest enemies in this world and never more so than when we are on the front lines of gospel ministry.

Notice the connection between spiritual warfare and prayer in Paul's instructions to the church at Ephesus:

> Put on the whole armor of God, that you may be able to stand against the schemes of the devil. For we do not wrestle against flesh and blood, but against the rulers, against the authorities, against the cosmic powers over this present darkness, against the spiritual forces of evil in the heavenly places. Therefore take up the whole armor of God, that you may be able to withstand in the evil day, and having done all, to stand firm. Stand therefore, having fastened on the belt of truth, and having put on the breastplate of righteousness, and, as shoes for your feet, having put on the readiness given by the gospel of peace. In all circumstances take up the shield of faith, with which you can extinguish all the flaming darts of the evil one; and take the helmet of salvation, and the sword of the Spirit, which is the word of God, praying at all times in the Spirit, with all prayer and supplication. To that end keep alert with all perseverance, making supplication for all the saints. (Eph. 6:11–18)

Pray for the scheme, housing project, trailer park, or council estate near your church. Pray hard and pray often. Pray for conversions. Very often we have not because we ask not. Whatever your thoughts are right now about being involved in gospel work among the poor, put this book down and get on your knees before God Almighty. That's the very best and most important thing you can do.

7. You Need to Understand Your Community

The perception of inner-city areas like schemes and council estates in the United Kingdom and the projects in the United States is primarily negative. When we hear about the Bronx or the east end of Glasgow, we may very well picture drug dealers and drive-by shootings. And this negativity is not without some roots in reality. These are places in the world with horrendous crime statistics, early deaths, drug offenses, and high infant mortality rates.

But that's not all there is to a community. If you move into an area and experience life firsthand—living, working, and socializing among local people—you may begin to see a rich tapestry of life and culture. The problem is that most of the thinking and writing about ministry among the poor is done by people who are well educated and at least middle class. That's not necessarily wrong. You don't have to come from a place to minister to a place. As I said before, what matters in the end is loving Jesus and people. But such love will show itself in taking care not to be led astray by your cultural assumptions. Many outreaches into poor communities lack fruit because the people doing the ministry do not really understand the culture and makeup of the particular area in which they are working, nor do they lovingly work to understand that area.

So if you are thinking about reaching an area near you, or if you have just moved into a difficult area, here are some questions to begin asking yourself and others (but be careful not to ask too many questions—people might start to think that you're working for the police!):

- What is your vision for a church in this community?
- Who are the key people you need to involve in the work? What are their gifts?
- Who do you want to reach? How will you reach them effectively?
- What other groups are at work in this community (secular or otherwise)? How effective are they?
- Who can help you learn more about your community?
- Is there somebody in this community who will offer you a "way in"?
- What kind of people do you naturally attract? Are these people in your community?
- What do people like to do in this community?
- Who do you need to recruit in order to attract people you cannot naturally reach?
- How will you build intentional relationships within your community? On your own? As a couple? As a small group?
- What is your plan for evangelism and discipleship?

If you do move into a needy area, pray regularly for it and study it deeply. Accept that there are a lot of things that you do not understand, and it will take a lot of time and effort and love before you ever do. But if you engage with people in their context, you will slowly but surely begin to build up a better understanding of the community. That will be invaluable in the coming years.

10

Prepare the Work

I (Mez) spent the first twelve months of my pastorate simply observing the community and getting to know the people of Niddrie Community Church. As the congregation's strengths and weakness became apparent, I realized that the church needed a completely new approach to ministry on the ground. We had a number of problems:

- We needed more elders, and we needed to understand what the role entailed.
- There was a "preach it and they will come" mentality to evangelism. Unsurprisingly, hardly any local people came.
- People expected the pastor to do most of the day-to-day ministry work.
- When I asked each member of the congregation to explain the mission and purpose of the church, I received as many different responses as we had people.
- The largely hostile community viewed the building and those who worshipped within it as an outsiders club.
- Many members were not utilizing their gifts for the benefit of the wider body.

We needed to move forward. But where to start? How do church planters, churches on the fringes of poor areas, or those feeling detached from poor communities take positive and practical steps forward in building healthy churches?

Build and Empower Godly Leadership

In my first few weeks at Niddrie Community, somebody asked me what model of hood I wanted for the church oven. I did not care in the slightest. I then began to teach the congregation that the pastor didn't need to be at every meeting and make every decision. Micromanaging does not equip people or build a team; delegating authority does. Consider the following verses from the Bible:

- "And he called the twelve and began to send them out two by two, and gave them authority over the unclean spirits." (Mark 6:7)
- "After this the Lord appointed seventy-two others and sent them on ahead of him, two by two, into every town and place where he himself was about to go." (Luke 10:1)
- "Two are better than one, because they have a good reward for their toil. For if they fall, one will lift up his fellow. But woe to him who is alone when he falls and has not another to lift him up!" (Eccles. 4:9–10)

1. Recruit and Train Elders

The church had elders, but two of them were aging and there didn't seem to be any clarity about the requirements of the role. If we were going to grow in a healthy way, we needed a strong, biblically informed eldership going forward. Over the next two years, I did the following:

- During my first twelve months I met individually with the men in the church to learn more about them.

- I began to give some of them opportunities to lead the Sunday meetings and midweek prayer meetings.
- I challenged them about the state of their souls and their walk with Jesus (a novelty for many of them).
- I observed who rose to the challenges of leading and who took a lead in praying during the midweek meetings or visiting the elderly or sick.
- I gave the men reading material on a host of issues—ecclesiology, the gospel, leadership, women in ministry—and encouraged thoughtful and healthy debate.
- We went out once or twice a month to socialize, sometimes just two of us and sometimes in groups. I wanted to see how the men interacted with one another.
- I prayed for the Lord to give me wisdom in moving forward.

After two years, I took a small group of men away for the day. They ranged in ages (twenties through sixties) and possessed a wide variety of gifts. We spent a full day together praying and talking about a number of doctrinal and theological issues. We studied the Scriptures and shared testimonies of how the Lord has saved us and brought us to this place. We discussed the following:

- The role of elders
- The state and future of Niddrie Community Church
- Evangelism
- Discipleship
- Church polity
- Training of future leaders

It was a great opportunity to see how these men interacted, and, importantly, how they disagreed with one another and resolved conflict in a biblical and mature fashion. Some were stronger theologically than others. Some were strong pastorally. Some lacked the ability to discuss doctrine in great depth but were humble learners. All fell within the qualifications of elder-ship as per 1 Timothy 3 and Titus 1. It was a great time and, one by one, as we took the vote to the congregation, the majority of these men were ordained as elders.

The dynamics of our elder meetings changed dramatically. We went from discussing problems like damaged doors and the lighting bill to grappling with pastoral issues, praying, and studying the Bible together. We read helpful books on church leadership and eldership.[1]

Perhaps the biggest turning point for us came in 2012 when our eldership attended a 9Marks conference in Washington, DC, called a "Weekender." With the blessing of the congregation we traveled to the United States and spent four full days observing the practices of Capitol Hill Baptist Church in Washington, DC. We each went to separate seminars, and in the evenings we pooled our knowledge together and decided what would work best for our context. The experience brought us closer together as brothers in Christ and undershepherds of God's people in Niddrie. Even though Capitol Hill Baptist Church and Niddrie Community Church were poles apart geographically and culturally, the principles we learned have had a profound effect on how we lead. The benefit to the church has been enormous.

- We began to meet as elders weekly instead of monthly.
- We use one meeting per month for our own personal study and pastoral interactions as leaders. We pray for one another and our families exclusively.
- We pray for our members twice per month.
- We began to teach not only about the need for membership but the nature of it. What responsibilities do leaders have? Members?

---

[1] Two extremely helpful books that helped us think about our role within the church were Alexander Strauch's *Biblical Eldership* (Colorado Springs: Lewis & Roth, 2003) and Mark Dever and Paul Alexander's *Deliberate Church* (Wheaton, IL: Crossway, 2005).

- We increased our members meetings from once per year to once per quarter.
- We developed and instituted a policy on church discipline that we have put into practice numerous times.

We now have an eldership that is growing together, learning together, holding one another spiritually accountable, and moving the church forward under the direction of God and his Word.

We'll talk more about preparing leaders in the next chapter.

2. Develop a Ministry Team

In the early days, most of our church members lived and worked outside of the scheme. I was quickly overwhelmed with discipling new believers and handling enquiries from people interested in the faith. Needy people were coming out of the woodwork. I needed help, but we didn't have enough Christians living in the community or indigenous converts mature enough for the job.

So I began by recruiting *cultural outsiders*. These were young Christian men and women from outside the schemes who wanted to learn about this kind of ministry but lacked the opportunity to get involved. I reasoned that raw recruits looking to serve the poor in parachurch organizations would be better served by coming to learn in Niddrie Community Church. Of course, I had to sell them on a vision for a local church that really would evangelize, disciple, and equip indigenous leaders and not just use and abuse them as glorified babysitters and youth workers. I needed to reassure them that they would have a voice in terms of new ministry initiatives. In other words, the elders wouldn't kill off every new idea and slow down progress through fear of change. Of course, the elders maintained oversight of everything, but they recognized that we would have to extend a lot of credit to our ministry team and allow them to make day-to-day decisions on the ground without too much interference.

Second, I recruited and trained *female workers*. In Scotland's poorest communities, 52 percent of all residents are single parents, the vast majority of whom are women. Women in the schemes suffer disproportionately from long-standing health problems, disability, and interpersonal violence. These are vulnerable and needy women with complex physical, psychological, and spiritual problems, and many of them sit in our pews.

These issues are not fixed by a weekly meeting over coffee. Helping these women requires a wholehearted life commitment to walk hand in hand with them. At the risk of stating the obvious, it's generally not wise or prudent for a man to counsel or invest significant amount of time into a woman's life. In the schemes, any form of tenderness from a male is likely to be misinterpreted sexually; a man with a listening ear is a powerful aphrodisiac.

Certainly, women need to be around examples of godly men and fathers. But the type of support, friendship, mentoring, intimacy in prayer, counsel, and care many women in the church need must come from biblically solid, mature women who are involved in their lives for the long haul. As a result, we must intentionally recruit and train women who can work in the ministry.

Third, I recruited only *people willing to make a long-term commitment*. Mike and I have both learned that ministry in hard places works only when we are prepared to put down roots. At Niddrie Community, each of my senior team members makes a ten- to fifteen-year commitment to the work. One of my church planters recently commented that when he was considering working with us, he asked himself if he was prepared to come and die on the scheme. Planting and revitalizing is not a smash-and-grab job. Fruit comes slowly in this kind of work.

We are seven years in, and we've only just begun to see the beginnings of real fruit. We must be in it for the long haul. We took a lot of risks in the early days. Some paid off, some didn't (more on that later). But young people are always attracted to vision. Vision helps people to imagine possibilities they might not have imagined before. It took a few years, but we eventually gathered momentum. The difference between ten people living in Niddrie and thirty is enormous.

Don't Be Defeated before You Even Start

Many church planters and established pastors wonder how they are going to get started when they are on their own or have very few resources. Many people come to Niddrie Community and comment that it's easier for us because we have a team. But we had nobody else working full time when I began the work. Start with the raw material you have and work from there. If you are on your own and starting from scratch, then pray for others to join you. Don't be in a rush. Choose team members carefully and be sure they understand your vision and direction. If you're an experienced pastor, then offer an internship to existing members or recruit from seminaries or other local churches. Maybe we do not have because we have not asked our heavenly Father. This is sure: change will not come if we are not willing to take steps of faith.

Don't Be Tied to One Model

Some people are passionate about one particular model for church planting and revitalizing, as if the job is best done the same way every time. But in my experience, there are a lot of good ways to go about it:

- In Brazil I started with a group of eight men and women. We met daily for a year, studying, praying, eating, and doing ministry on the streets together. When the time came to start a work in our favela, we knew each other very well and we hit the ground running. The church grew quickly.

- In Niddrie I inherited a group, and so I had to go about reeducating them, largely from the pulpit. I invested more time with those who seemed like they resonated with the new vision for ministry. It has been a different way of doing church but it is slowly becoming effective.

- In Dundee, 20Schemes has helped to place a church planter in an old church building that closed its doors nearly two decades ago. Situated in a needy community of eighteen thousand people, the building has been used by a number of youth and children's ministries for the last ten years. The work requires a leader with the ability to draw people together and form a coherent vision.

- In an Edinburgh scheme called Gracemount, 20Schemes has placed a young couple who are trying to start a church from scratch. They have contacts through a local parachurch ministry, but the leader here needs entrepreneurial gifts, evangelistic ability, and a solid team to build momentum. This will be a slow-burning ministry.

- In Glasgow, two young couples have moved onto a scheme after working there for over five years as youth workers. They will need help and guidance and the support and accountability of another established church as they seek to plant a local gospel church in the scheme.

- Mike's church has had similar experiences. They have revitalized, planted from scratch, sent out a good-sized team, and started churches for speakers of other languages using evangelistic Bible studies.

The point is that there is no one perfect way to do planting and revitalizing. Every location is different and presents different opportunities. A trailer park might require a different strategy than an urban housing project, both of which might be very different from a church plant in the suburbs. If you are tied to one model, you may miss a good opportunity. If you import your model into a different location without taking into account its culture and needs, you are asking for trouble.

Be Realistic about the Financial Cost

Two young men made an appointment to see me in my office to talk about their vision of working with gangs in South Africa. When I asked them how much money they were hoping to raise, the answer was naively low. Apparently they planned to live on a shoestring without factoring in rent, car, fuel, a work fund, getting home, medical expenses, and a little luxury called food. They had absolutely no clue about the true cost of what they were trying to do. Most churches and planters are not quite that naive, but many have little clue about the costs associated with planting or revitalizing churches in poor areas.

The average Western church-planting strategy plans for financial independency in three to five years. That is extremely unrealistic in poor communities where fiscal independency may take a decade or more. New ministries to the poor require a missionary effort and long-term financing. Thinking carefully about financial issues can help protect the church planter from worry, preoccupation, and anxiety.

The difficulty of financing a church in poor areas is one reason why churches everywhere should join or develop a close network with other churches. Together they can financially and spiritually support the work of churches in poorer areas. If you are part of an affluent church looking to help see the gospel spread among the poor, it may be that the most effective way for your congregation to participate is through financial support. We also need to cultivate individual donors who appreciate and understand the context of our ministry. Sadly, these kinds of people are in short supply in a world that likes quick results and statistics-heavy newsletters with amazing conversion stories. In light of that fact, our strategy has been to approach ministry among the poor as a long-term missionary endeavor. We encourage our workers to raise financial support in order to create sustainability.

Have Realistic Goals and Expectations

I remember sitting in a meeting in New York and hearing a church planter say that if we are not seeing 200 people in our plant by the third year, then maybe we ought to question our call. Another planter told us he was moving in faith to a new area with a core team of 150 people. We once had some American church planters visit our service in Niddrie where we had about seventy-five people in attendance. Afterward, during lunch, one of them said that he thought we would be more successful if we had better musicians and brightened the place up a bit. I informed him that in housing scheme terms, we are a megachurch! It seems that Europe and the United States are often different when it comes to attitudes toward fruitfulness and success.

When I hear stories of churches attracting many hundreds to their launch services, I assume that most of the people in attendance are Christians who have been part of other churches in the area. A church in a poor community is far less likely to have a large reservoir of Christians to draw from. It is likely to grow more slowly because it will have to grow through conversions. Certainly, God could send revival and shower us with thousands of converts. But barring something extraordinary, I will be delighted if we see pockets of twenty to forty believers in multiple schemes after ten years of work. That would constitute great success, even though it might seem like a core group to some! Frankly, we put far too much pressure on our church planters and revitalizers with unrealistic goals and expectations.

Conclusion

All new converts and members of a congregation, regardless of their social status, must be taught about their responsibility to their local body. Some will make great members of ministry teams. Some may make good deacons. Some will be godly elders. But their gifts will come to light only if they are given opportunities to test themselves in the fires of ministry. The same is true of our women. Many godly and biblically mature women are sitting on the shelf, largely unused by churches, when there is a huge need for them in hard places.

The bottom line is that churches in hard places, like all places, must cultivate cultures of discipleship and ministry, where the members, leaders, and would-be leaders learn to disciple one another and understand such activity to be an ordinary part of being a Christian. This way they learn to serve, to fail, to forgive, to encourage, and to learn from one another.

11

Prepare to Change Your Thinking

Imagine that a young man walks into your church one day and asks to speak to the pastor. He has been in trouble with the law since he was a child and just finished a prison sentence for robbery and serious assault. He looks agitated and goes outside the building for a smoke while you try to find the pastor. He smells like he hasn't washed in a while, and his clothes look cheap and shabby.

It turns out that this young man recently made a profession of faith in Christ, and though he's never read a Bible in his life, he wants to come to your church to find out more about Jesus. He is currently living in a homeless shelter in town, and he admits to drug use, but he claims that he is trying to quit. He is quite aggressive and clearly doesn't like being asked a lot of questions.

What would you be thinking as this young man walked away? Would you secretly hope that he wouldn't come back? Would you wonder who will manage him if he returns on Sunday? Would you think about how to help him get out of the shelter and off of drugs? Would you think *disciple* or *disaster*?

It's my (Mez) contention that what you may have on your hands is a future leader. If you are going to do church ministry among the poor, then you will need to see that this dirty, aggressive, biblically illiterate young man might potentially be a future pastor and leader in the church. The question is: does your church have a clear discipleship pathway for these kinds of young men and women? Or are these kinds of people tolerated until they drift back to their old life, and then everyone breathes a secret sigh of relief?

The Problem in Our Churches

The truth is, many churches lack a culture of discipleship for converts from poor backgrounds. These kinds of people may be welcomed into our congregations, but they are usually overlooked when it comes to identifying and training potential leaders. This is not a new problem; forty years ago the Lausanne Covenant highlighted the same issue:

> We also acknowledge that some of our missions have been too slow to equip and encourage national leaders to assume their rightful responsibilities. Yet we are committed to indigenous principles, and long that every church will have national leaders who manifest a Christian style of leadership in terms not of domination but of service. We recognise that there is a great need to improve theological education, especially for church leaders. In every nation and culture there should be an effective training programme for pastors and laity in doctrine, discipleship, evangelism, nurture and service. Such training programmes should not rely on any stereotyped methodology but should be developed by creative local initiatives according to biblical standards.

The problem that the authors of the Lausanne Covenant were addressing was the tendency for Western missionaries to cripple indigenous churches abroad by failing to raise up leaders in culturally sensitive ways. In a similar way, it is easy for churches in the West to fall behind the curve when it comes to training leaders among its own poor. If you don't believe me, read the advertisements in the Christian press for church interns; you will see that they are almost exclusively for educated people. The fact is, leadership in many churches is the sole domain of the formally educated and the professionally qualified.

Leaders in established positions can too easily project the sense that only they have the skills and knowledge necessary for leadership. We can subtly communicate that only the cleaned-up and impressive people can be considered for Christian leadership. Surely an elder must be "able to teach," but formal education and business savvy are not qualifications for Christian leadership (see 1 Tim. 3:1–13). In fact, a church's leadership models should look somewhat different from the world's leadership models because God values different things than the world does (1 Cor. 1:26–29). Churches and institutional leaders need to stop overlooking those who lack professional qualifications or who don't fit into their social circle.

A Fresh Approach

We need to rethink how we do ministry in the hard places of our towns and cities. Having a heart for the poor and the downtrodden is all well and good, but we need to watch out for the sort of disabling help that provides assistance to people in poor communities but never offers them the help that they need to become mature disciples of Christ.

Let me give you an example. At a recent discussion on ministry to the poor, I mentioned that one of the problems with mercy ministries was that they failed to help grow indigenous leadership among the poor. One man took exception, claiming that their church's soup kitchen had transformed their community. When we drilled down into the specifics, however, it seemed that most of the benefit from the soup kitchen had been experienced in the church. Fringe members had discovered that distributing food was an easy way to become engaged in ministry. That is a good thing. But the man also admitted that, after a significant amount of time doing this ministry, there were still no conversions and no one being discipled. Worse, there were no plans in place if someone did become a Christian.

Mercy ministry is great if it is part of a bigger plan, but it cannot be the end of the story for those receiving help. So what *is* the way forward? Churches that are working with the poor must incorporate training indigenous leaders into their DNA.

So how do we get from our dire situation on the ground today to the future ideals of indigenous leadership? In the schemes of Scotland we have come to terms with the fact that we are going to have to rely on "cultural outsiders" to help us at first. There is not enough in place right now to develop any significant momentum toward indigenous leadership. We will have to train these "outsiders" to identify and cultivate "insiders" who can serve as future leaders. Perhaps within a generation we will see a real movement toward churches in the schemes being led by converts from the schemes.

Toward that end, here are ten suggestions that arise out of my experience training men and women for leadership in poor communities:

1. Give New Converts Responsibility Quickly
Often middle-class community churches will wait for new converts to prove themselves before giving them any leadership roles. In the schemes, we have found that it's better to give peo-

ple responsibility and let them run with it until they prove themselves to be unable. In other words, it's good to give converts responsibility quickly and release them into areas of service and teaching. I'm not talking about making them elders, but I'm not just talking about chair stacking either. And our equipping cannot be limited to lectures from the front of the room. We need to walk with them in the day-in and day-out work of ministry. After all, that is how Jesus trained his disciples; they did life together, and he taught them along the way.

At Niddrie Community Church we have a young worker who has been saved for a very short time. She is a local girl who came to us with no previous knowledge of the Bible. Within two months of her conversion, we decided to employ her part-time to reach out to young people in the area. Before long, she started a Bible study with five friends. She knew hardly anything except the gospel, but within weeks some of her pals were attending the church and a couple were saved. She made more progress locally in six months than we had in six years! We simply had a mature Christian woman sit in on her Bible studies to offer help and advice if our young lady got stuck. With this culture of freedom, she has gone on to start other ministries within the community, while simultaneously being trained through our in-house training program.

2. Communicate in Culturally Sensitive Ways
Communication is contextual. For example, in the schemes we value straight talking; it is a sign of respect in our relationships. Middle-class people tend to place a higher value on not giving offense; it's how they communicate that they care about the relationship. As a result, one side looks rude and aggressive to the other, whereas the other appears wishy-washy and superficial. We must be careful to understand how people speak and act before questioning their motivation or character. Many hous-

ing scheme converts are overlooked for leadership because they can appear gauche, rude, and aggressive in comparison to their middle-class brothers and sisters. Understanding the culture of your location can help with some of that and take the edge off. We must, of course, challenge sinful behavior whatever our culture, but I fear that many potential leaders are written off because of misunderstandings about the way that people in different cultures communicate.

3. Embrace Failure as an Opportunity

We are sometimes so puffed up with pride that we think if a person we are discipling falls or goes back to his or her old ways, it is somehow a black mark against us or our ministry. But honestly, if we are not failing, then we are not growing. We are going to make some mistakes with leadership.

Jesus gave the early disciples room to fail. They often learned in the heat of battle. And so we also must loosen the reigns and fight the fear that our disciples are not ready for ministry. That fear is a killer on the mission field; it locks down ministry. There's a time for caution and a time to take risks.

4. Look for Unlikely Leaders

Some of us lack faith in the power of the gospel and the Holy Spirit to transform unlikely people. Take another look at that diamond in the rough, that person in your congregation who seems like he or she is not even close to leadership material. Invest some time in them, and God might just surprise you. But the one thing we can be sure of is that if we keep waiting for leaders in poor communities who look like respectable middle-class Christians, we will be waiting a long time.

I've heard amazing stories of people who turned around dying churches and now have thousands of members. I've been awed by church planters in India who have planted dozens of churches while still in their early twenties. But honestly I am just as interested in those who have tried and failed.

I met one such young man a few years ago. He turned up at my church, and I learned that he was part of a failed international church planting team in Asia. Ten people had joined together to plant an international church, and one by one they had given up and gone home. In the end, he was the only one left. When I met him, he was a bit beaten up and defeated. After I heard his story, I hired him almost immediately.

Failure is the breeding ground for humility. Lots of young planters are feisty and proud because they have not yet been stung by defeat. I was impressed by the fact that this man was the last person standing on his team. That told me everything I needed to know about his persevering spirit. After he trained with me for a year, his faith was renewed and his confidence restored. He also taught my team some invaluable lessons.

Some of the most profitable conversations I have had were with people who were struggling (or failing!) in hard places. I know men who have had to try several times to plant or revitalize churches before they saw lasting fruit. I know others who have given up and returned back to the workplace. I intentionally seek these people out because the mistakes they made and the lessons they learned are of great value to me.

As you think about recruiting a team, don't just go for the super savvy, pumped-up seminary graduate, but look for people who have been beaten up a bit. They tend to make first-rate team members.

5. Treat It Like Cross-Cultural Ministry

If you are an outsider going into ministry among the poor, you must come to grips with the fact that you are going into cross-cultural work. Don't make the mistake of thinking that you share cultural values with someone just because you are from the same country and speak the same language. In fact, I think that before you think about working on a scheme or in a project, you should get some cross-cultural experience. It will force you to ask difficult questions of yourself and your own cultural preferences, and it might show you your blind spots. Hopefully, all of that will drive you to seek biblical solutions as you operate outside your natural bounds.

People and places are not fundamentally things that need to be fixed. If you come into a poor community with anything other than love and appreciation, you are sunk before you begin. Its damage and difficulties may look different than your home community's damage and difficulties, but every culture has them. We just see others' problems more clearly. Our job is not to fix whole cultures, but to share the good news and to disciple those God draws to himself. We must be watchful for our ethnocentricities.

We also have to work hard to learn the culture into which we are moving. The apostle Paul spent time walking through Athens before he preached to the people on Mars Hill. In the same way, we must faithfully observe the culture around us; we can't assume that we understand anything. We need to be constant questioners:

- What are some of the strengths and weaknesses of the culture we are engaging with?
- What are our own strengths and weaknesses?
- What biblical principles transcend both cultures?

6. Embrace Conflict as an Opportunity

Most people do not like conflict, and that makes sense. Tension, frustration, and sharp words make day-to-day life less pleasant. But when we begin to structure our teams in order to avoid conflict, we have a problem. The diversity of opinions, skills, and backgrounds that are required to build an effective team will create an environment where people are prone to misunderstandings and disagreements. But we don't want to value tranquility to the point that we employ only yes-men and yes-women. We want strong, free thinkers who ultimately submit to authority but push the team and ministry forward.

If you build teams with sinful human beings, you will experience conflict. This is especially true if you are mixing cultural insiders and outsiders. Every week people are in my office with issues: they have misunderstood each other, misread the motivations of others, and communicated their own true feelings and intentions poorly. This is normal and not to be avoided. It should be used instead as an opportunity to resolve problems and explore the heart issues that lie beneath the surface.

When conflict between team members is handled well, everyone benefits. Difficulties are resolved instead of swept under the carpet, mature Christians will grow in patience, and young believers will learn how we resolve disagreements in a constructive and godly way. The sanctification process blesses all.

7. Develop Culturally Relevant Models of Theological Training

Most churches expect that theological training will be done in seminaries and Bible colleges. And while that system has many benefits, it usually works against people from impoverished backgrounds. It simply is not an effective model for training the numbers of indigenous believers needed for ministry in poorer areas. Most would not be granted admission, and many would not want to go or be able to afford to go even if they were accepted.

Instead, we need to return to grassroots theological education tailored for one's particular context and driven by the local church. If churches will embrace the responsibility, they are in a great position to combine doctrinal education with practical missiological application and personal character development. We need to work out how to combine contextualized theological education that is helpful for our people and is retained, governed, and assessed on the ground by the local church.

8. Establish Multicultural Teams

Given the ever-changing face of Western societies, it is hard to find a common cultural core in many places. A poor community is often a mix of people from all kinds of backgrounds: the long-term "underclass," middle-class people looking to gentrify a neighborhood, working-class people, and a growing immigrant community. Many neighborhoods are an interesting hodgepodge of humanity.

In order to reach diverse places, we should develop multicultural teams. These kinds of teams may have some inefficiencies (see the section on conflict above), but they will be stronger and more effective in the long run. Diverse teams have fewer blind spots and a greater variety of experiences, expectations, and personalities. They can connect naturally with a larger portion of the community. Whether we like it or not, like does attract like, and there is nothing stronger than a team made of different people types and personalities working together for the glory of the gospel.

9. Be Aware of Your Personal Biases about Behavior

We must be careful to make sure that our leadership development draws lines where the Bible does. If a young man or woman is converted out of a lifestyle of drug abuse and immorality and then moves toward ministry leadership, what are realistic expectations for their behavior?

- Is it okay for them to wear a track suit to church?
- Do they need to stop smoking?
- Do they need to speak like an educated person?
- Do they need to express praise to God in a certain way?

We must begin to disentangle what the Bible says from our personal cultural preferences. Smoking is stupid, but I am not sure it is always a sin. Look at any picture of a seminary faculty from the 1940s; almost every professor will be holding a cigarette. But many middle-class people will condemn those who waste their money on cigarettes, all the while indulging a $100-a-month Starbucks habit. We need to work hard at ensuring we build our teams on the gospel, not primarily on law and certainly not our cultural ideals. Sin must be challenged, of course, but we must trust the Holy Spirit of God to bring about real conviction in someone's life. If we don't, then we will be left with judgmentalism, distrust, and a lack of love, understanding, and patience among us.

10. Be Honest about the Cost

Churches in poor communities cannot afford to exist only on Sunday mornings. Coming to Christ in the schemes is costly; it is often akin to someone who converts from Islam. The convert's family and friends and business partners may not say much at first, expecting that this newfound religion is just a fad. But as time goes on, opposition will rise up against the individual and the church. When a drug dealer or prostitute comes to Christ, lives may well be at risk. Pimps, gang members, and abusive partners do not take well to losing people who have been serving their purposes.

And so new believers need more than just a weekly meeting. They need a new family. They need to be able to hang out with us, question us, and pray with us daily. They are going to experience an onslaught of spiritual attack from Satan, and they will need their brothers and sisters next to them in the dark moments. Discipleship without deep friendship is merely club membership.

Conclusion

Whether we are engaged in pioneering planting, revitalization, or pastoring in hard places, we need biblical, gospel-centered elders who can model spiritual health and growth for the congregation. Obviously, if your congregation has no elders, or positively resists elders, this is difficult. Still, as soon as possible, make the transition to eldership.

For example, Ian, a church planter in a hard place in England, leads a small group of new Christians seeking to establish a local church. Because he lacks any mature male believers, he has partnered with Niddrie Community Church and has voluntarily submitted himself to the accountability of our eldership team until he is able to grow, disciple, and train his own eldership. This is good for him because (1) it gives him mutual support and encouragement from godly, experienced brothers, and (2) it protects this fledging group from becoming dominated by his personality and views. He has a wider sounding board from a group of men to whom he can come before making major decisions on his own. Importantly, it protects his group from becoming overly dependent on him and buys him the time he needs to think about how to develop his discipleship and leadership training as people respond to Christ's call upon their lives.

Mike and I understand that we don't have everything right. We hope that sharing some of our mistakes, experiences, and hints picked up along the way will help you. But we acknowledge that practice often falls short of principle and, on this side of heaven at least, the reality on the ground will never match the ideals in our heads. It's easier to write about these things than to live in the grit of them. But our hope is that whatever your gifts, experiences, and opportunities may be, you will prayerfully consider how you can be part of seeing the gospel spread through the local church in hard places.

12

Prepare for Mercy Ministry?

Honestly, we did not want to write this chapter. For most evangelicals thinking about ministry among the poor, the conversation begins and ends with deeds of practical service and benevolence. If a church operates mercy ministries, offering things like a food pantry or a clothes closet or backpacks of food for local school children, the assumption is that they are reaching the poor about as well as you can.

Part of our purpose in this book is to move mercy ministries out of the middle of the conversation. We want the gospel and the local church to occupy that place of privilege because we think they occupy that place in the Bible's plan to reach the world for Christ. So, something of the contrarian in us wanted to make a statement simply by not mentioning mercy ministries at all. But we do feel that organized acts of practical care can play a role in a church seeking to reach a needy community, and so at the risk of getting away from our larger purpose, here are some things that you need to wrestle with before you open a soup kitchen in your church.

The Church Has a Mission

The risen Christ gave his people a mission: in the power of the Holy Spirit, they were to preach the gospel and form churches out of the new believers. In Matthew 28:19–20, Jesus sends his disciples out to make disciples of the nations and to teach them to obey (see chap. 3 for more on this). In Acts 1:8, he tells his people to serve as his witnesses to the end of the earth. So while a church may do a lot of different things in the service of that mission, everything that it does should be aimed at those final goals: proclaiming the gospel and helping people to grow in their obedience to God. Starbucks sells coffee, Listerine makes mouthwash, and the church holds out the gospel and trains people to obey by doing the work of ministry. If we don't do it, no one will. If we do anything else, we are getting off track.[1]

Mercy Ministries Can Serve the Mission of the Church

Mercy ministries can be a helpful way for a congregation to fulfill that mission. For example, they can provide an opportunity for people to obey Jesus is practical ways. As people's hearts are captured by the compassion of Christ, part of their growth in godliness may well take the form of increased care for the physical and emotional burdens of needy people. After all, the Bible is full of instructions for Christians to be caring, generous, and merciful people. In that sense, a food pantry ministry or a drug and alcohol recovery program may be the fruit of a church full of Christians obeying Jesus.

Deeds of mercy can also show the power of the gospel to change us. When we help our neighbor, we give evidence that

---

[1] For a thorough defense of this idea (along with a healthy dose of the delights and glories of free-market capitalism), see Kevin DeYoung and Greg Gilbert's *What Is the Mission of the Church? Making Sense of Social Justice, Shalom, and the Great Commission* (Wheaton, IL: Crossway, 2011).

our message is true. If we claim that the gospel has the power to change lives, then our mercy is one of the things that proves it. In a world where most people keep to themselves and only take care of their own, Christians have an opportunity to stun others with our inexplicable love and selfless service.

When we help others in practical ways, we are acknowledging that God created us as physical beings. The state of our flesh greatly impacts our lives. Life is more difficult when we are hungry, cold, intoxicated, sick, or in danger. And so evangelistic proclamation that doesn't recognize the physical factors at work in the lives of its hearers risks being tone-deaf and insensitive. It is important that we recognize that there is an order to our needs, and that sometimes our greatest needs are not our most immediate needs. So we can say with confidence that the greatest need of every human being is to be reconciled to God through faith in Christ. But if someone comes to your door with a gaping head wound, that need, though lesser, must be tended to. First you must take care of the head wound, and then you should share the gospel.

It's also important to recognize that mercy ministries can generate opportunities to share the gospel. We all like to be around people who are kind to us, who take an interest in our lives, and who demonstrate a desire to help us. So showing practical care to others is an easy way to build bridges into your community. A few examples from Mike's church:

- A church planter ministering among the working poor takes a few bags of food with him when he goes to visit people in their homes. The gift goes a long way toward cementing a friendship in which the gospel can be shared.
- People from the church help desperately poor children at a local elementary school. The church members build relationships with the students and their families and invite them to get involved with a church plant in their area.

- A group of at-risk teenagers are hosted at the church each week. They get a meal, a chance to hang out with their friends in a safe environment, and an opportunity to build relationships with positive adult role models. Each week they hear a lesson from the Bible that presses the gospel into their lives.

Of course, we should all be sharing Christ with the people whose lives naturally intersect with ours, such as neighbors, friends, and coworkers. But moving toward needy people with deeds of mercy provides opportunities to build relationships with those with whom we might not otherwise come into contact.

Mercy Ministries Are Dangerous

With that said, we are very wary of the way that many churches approach their mercy ministries. Frankly, most churches that wander into the wilds of helping the poor in practical ways wind up doing more harm than good. While this is not the case in every situation, here are some of the things that we have seen on the ground that give us pause:

1. *Mercy ministries are easily abused.* I (Mez) lived on the streets in my late teens and early twenties. I could always find places that would give me breakfast, clean clothes, a shower, and some food. Those of us who lived and breathed within this largely invisible subculture knew how to play the system. We knew exactly what to do and say in order to get the things that we wanted with minimum engagement. Churches were particularly good targets because the people were generally nice, they would be kind to you, they were less savvy than government agencies, and all we had to do was sit through some God-talk and maybe take a booklet. Then we could be on our way. The constant stream of questions could be annoying, but

once we figured out what the church people wanted to hear, we could easily placate them. They would get to say their bit about God and be nice to a poor person, and we would get what we wanted. What looked like a thriving mercy ministry was really just an easy mark for selfish people.

2. *Mercy ministries support sin.* While this is not true of everyone, we have to be honest: a significant portion of the people who avail themselves of church mercy ministries are living in sinful lifestyles. Feeding a lazy man simply encourages his sin and enables him to avoid the consequences of his actions. Giving clothes to a drug addict may simply provide him with something to sell in order to buy his next fix. Providing shelter to a homeless person might remove his motivation to reconcile with his family.

If you give a man a fish, not only will he be back the next day looking for more, but you run the risk of reinforcing the very problems that caused him to come looking for a handout in the first place. In other words, it is one thing to give food to a person who is working (or who wants to work but is unable) and is just plain hungry. It is another thing to give food to a person whose sin compels him *not* to work, but to look for the handout because he thinks he deserves it. In this latter situation, you are actually at risk of affirming and enabling people in their sin, and therefore you are unwittingly encouraging their sin.

3. *Mercy ministries can be paternalistic and self-serving.* If we are honest, most mercy ministries do not accomplish much beyond making the people who run it feel good about themselves. Most church mercy ministries are run by middle-class people who love Jesus, and often these people are motivated by a mixture of godly intentions and misplaced guilt. Instead of actually helping people, too many mercy ministries are content

to do things that merely appear to help people. The end result is a program that makes people dependent on handouts and help from the people who are "above" them on the social ladder. Not much enduring fruit comes from these ministries, but no one wants to cut them lest they seem unconcerned about the poor.

Canadian antipoverty activist Nick Saul caused a stir worldwide with the following statement about food banks. He criticized them for being about "privileged people helping the underprivileged, perpetuating an us-and-them atmosphere."[2] Saul believes that traditional food banks don't really help the needy. The food they provide is often poor quality, and the process does nothing to help clients' dignity or self-esteem, get them a job, help them out of poverty, or improve their health and well being. People's immediate hunger is satisfied, but that doesn't last long. Here is his haunting commentary on most food bank initiatives: "The only person who is not benefiting is the person who this was set up to help. Most people who have to visit food banks say it is a slow, painful death of the soul."[3]

Few things are sadder in the world than seeing a regular at a soup kitchen. It is a travesty. Very often, the people are not being moved on to dignified self-sufficiency; they are not being really helped. They are not being challenged and equipped to help themselves. And so we have to ask: if these mercy ministries are not really meeting the needs of the poor, whose needs are they meeting?

4. *Mercy ministries foster mission creep.* Perhaps the greatest danger is that mercy ministries can distract a church from its main mission. Mercy ministries are attractive service opportunities for Christians. You can probably get twice as many

[2] Patrick Butler, "Food Banks Are 'a Slow Death of the Soul,'" *theguardian*, September 25, 2013. http://www.theguardian.com/society/2013/sep/25/food-banks-slow-death-soul/.
[3] Ibid.

volunteers to show up for a workday in a soup kitchen as would come to training on how to do evangelism. After all, the world will applaud us for feeding the poor. Feeding the poor makes us feel good about ourselves; maybe (if we are honest) it even makes us feel like we are better than all of the other people who did not show up to help. But evangelism and discipleship don't always come with that same burst of satisfaction. Oftentimes they will mean rejection and awkward conversations. There is a real temptation to be content with merely meeting physical needs. But that is the tail wagging the dog.

But what poor people need most is the gospel of Jesus Christ (see chap. 1), and the church is the means by which the gospel is proclaimed. If we do not do it, it will not happen. And so any church working in poor areas must be vigilant to make sure that it does not get sidetracked by its relief work.

Doing Mercy Ministry Well Is Difficult and Time-Consuming

As we have said, we are not opposed to mercy ministries. We are simply saying that if we are going to operate them, we have to do so in a way that makes sense of the mission of the church. But if we are going to do that, we have to be prepared to invest a lot of time and effort.

Mercy ministry needs to be done in the context of relationships and accountability. No accountability structure works perfectly; there will always be people who game the system. We are not suggesting that you wait to start a mercy ministry until you can be 100 percent sure that people will not take advantage of you. But if there should be any difference between the state and the church's version of a handout, it's that the church should distribute its handouts in the context of relationships with Christians.

This will look different from context to context, and maybe

different from season to season in your family's life. But no matter what, this means Christians will have to sacrifice *time*, because relationships are time-intensive. It seems so much easier just to donate canned goods and feel better about ourselves, doesn't it? But we are called to donate time as well. In my (Mike) own life, this has involved things like hosting a weekly dinner and Bible study for homeless people and playing soccer with Latin American teenagers.

When the Lord blesses our efforts and we see evangelistic fruit from our efforts, we have to be ready to disciple new converts and help them to engage and minister fully in the life of the congregation. But if we have started a mercy ministry with no plan beyond the crisis-intervention stage, we will never get beyond the very first stages of discipleship with a needy person. And so churches need to think through the long-term ramifications of their ministry to the poor. We must think about what we are going to do with somebody who comes to faith through a mercy ministry. What is the discipleship strategy? Who will care for them? Who will hold them accountable? How will we move them forward in their walk with Jesus? How will we prepare them for whatever works of service God has called them to once he has saved them? How will we identify and train the former drug dealers and homeless people and sexual predators that the Lord is calling into full-time ministry?

At Niddrie Community Church, the Holy Spirit of God is at work in bringing many to faith from the wider community. The church structure has a clear path from evangelism to early discipleship and on to God-honoring service either back in the workplace or in vocational ministry. Some in the internship training program have been sexually abused, abandoned, addicted, or written off as mentally ill; others come from stable and loving backgrounds. Of the people the church is training theologically, at least two-thirds come from a background of addiction, homelessness, mental illness, or abuse.[4] In fact, Mez himself is a product of a local church heavily investing in his life *after* they had reached out to him on the streets and he had spent time in prison.

This is really the heart of the matter. Are we content to feed hungry people? That's nice, but it is less than full Christian love. Are we content to share the gospel with people? That's even better than food, but still not the end of the work. No, Christian love desires to see in people's lives the same thing that God desires to see in them: wholehearted fruitful, faithful obedience to Christ. So count the cost. If you are not willing to invest the time to see the job all the way through, you are probably best off not starting a mercy ministry.

Conclusion

There are different kinds of "hard places," and churches need to understand theirs. In a place like Scotland, where generations of people have been raised and sustained on welfare handouts, we find a strong mentality of entitlement. A church there is at great risk of enabling people in their sin of exploiting others. A church might decide to hand out fish, but it might also decide to do the counterintuitive thing of only handing out the fishing pole of the gospel, not fish, at least programmatically. Elders and members will hand out fish personally and privately, but that forces the handouts to always occur in the context of relationships. That way, when you encounter the teenage versions of Mez, you'll give him a lunch, but he'll have to eat it with you!

The immigrants of Northern Virginia, on the other hand, possess a strong work ethic, but pressing needs back home, low wages, and inconsistent opportunities often conspire to create acute poverty. A church in that context (like Mike's) might

---

[4] For more on what this looks like practically, visit 20Schemes.com.

have more opportunity to show the love of Christ by handing out both fish and fishing poles. If you are going to run a mercy ministry in the church, you need to prayerfully consider your context, constantly evaluate the work that you are doing, and be willing to adjust in light of the realities on the ground.

As we said, we were reluctant to write this chapter. We realize that writing anything negative about mercy ministries means that we are likely to come off as Republicans (which we are not) and jerks (which only one of us is). But we genuinely do not think that our message is unloving or ungracious. We are very grateful for the people who sacrificially serve the practical needs of the poor, homeless, mentally ill, and other "at-risk" people in our neediest communities. These people are to be applauded and supported by all pastors and Christians. We simply do not want to see the church become focused on meeting practical needs and thus get sidetracked from the entirety of its gracious mission.

Conclusion

Count the Cost . . . and Reward

Let me (Mike) tell you two stories. A few years ago, my wife and I were considering becoming foster parents. Working with at-risk kids in our community had produced the burden in us to be a safe place for children living in terrible circumstances. Some of the young people that we had formed relationships with through the church had babies of their own, and in light of their living conditions and general lack of support at home, we found ourselves having regular conversations with Child Protective Services about the welfare of both the mothers and the babies. Becoming foster parents seemed like a great way for us to connect with our mission field. After all, when CPS felt like they needed to remove a child in our neighborhood from his or her home, they could place the child with us. We already had a relationship (or at least a relatively few degrees of relational separation) with many of these families, and so the thinking was that placing a child with us might be less traumatic for the family and a good opportunity for us to engage people with the gospel.

As this idea began to gain traction, Karen and I sought counsel from others in our church. A lot of responses were along the lines of what you might expect—somewhere between mildly encouraging ("I think that's great") to mildly discouraging ("Do you really think you have the room in your life for that?"). But on the whole, people offered to support us if we decided to go forward with it.

But one type of reaction really struck home. Boiled down to its essence, it was this: "Why do you hate your children so much?" One person spoke at length about how he could not bear how his own children would feel betrayed and neglected if he brought a needy foster child into the home. Another asked how we could think about introducing ungodliness and dysfunction into the fragile ecosystem of our family. Yet another worried that we were sacrificing the well-being of our five children on the altar of ministry ambitions.

I am by (fallen?) nature a contrarian. If you tell me that I cannot or should not do something and then give me a garbage reason for your thinking, then you'll make me want to do it 1,000 percent more. But my wife has a heart and a conscience, and she was far more impacted by such criticisms. After all, there was a kernel of truth there. Having a foster child would certainly impact our kids. There would be additional stresses on our time and money; there might be significant and troubling behavior issues. We could think of no scenario in which introducing a stranger into the tight-knit fabric of our family would not cost our kids something.

So how were we to make a decision? On one hand, we had the (doubtlessly over-romanticized) vision of stepping in to save a child in dire circumstances. On the other hand, we faced the (doubtlessly overly fearful) possibility that our kids would grow up to hate Jesus and eventually get their revenge by leaving us to die in a substandard nursing home.

In the end, we wound up becoming foster parents. Soon after, a teenager from Central America was placed with us. Her stepfather back home had sold her to some men in a neighboring state (in the United States); she managed to break out of the room where she was being held, and had been living in the youth homeless shelter in a town near us. She lived with us for six months, and in truth it was really hard. She spoke no English, and we speak no Spanish. She was a sweet kid, but she had a temper. Our kids were little at the time, and having a teenager in the house was a shock to the system. There were tears.

But it was also really good. This young woman heard the gospel over and over. She saw it lived out in the life of our family and in our church. She received physical and emotional care for perhaps the first time in her life. There is no doubt that she will need to continue swimming upstream for the foreseeable future. But I have no doubt that the Lord used us to accomplish his purposes in her life. I walked away from that experience thinking, "I'm really glad that we did that."

Okay, so now another story. A while after that young lady left our home, the county called again. This time, they needed to place an eleven-year-old boy with autism. His home environment was erratic, and he wasn't getting the medical or dental care that he needed. In a nurturing and stable environment, he might well be able to grow and develop into someone who could function in wider society. But as it was, the neglect and abuse at home were serving to push him deeper into himself.

Again, we decided to seek counsel. At a monthly lunch for our church's elders and their wives and children, we told everyone what we were contemplating. These are our closest partners in ministry, the men and women whose wisdom we trust more than any others. And they were unanimous in their counsel: we should not accept this opportunity. Lovingly, they pointed out all of the ways in which our lives were already stretching toward the breaking point. They brought up all of the pressing needs in the church, the demands of our own children, and a whole host of stressors that had developed in our lives since our last experience with foster care. To them it was clear that this was not a wise idea.

That night, Karen and I processed the lunchtime conversation. The county needed an answer the next morning and, as we prayed and talked about it, we decided to accept the placement. It gave us pause to go against the counsel of people we trusted, but we felt like we needed to be willing to pay the price to serve Christ and serve needy people. Karen has significant medical experience, and it seemed like we were particularly qualified to help this helpless child. How could we turn him away? We went to bed that night determined that I would call the county in the morning and make arrangements to have the child placed in our home the following week.

When I woke up the next morning, the first postcoffee thought that popped into my mind was, "What are we thinking? We can't do this." I was suddenly absolutely certain that this was a terrible idea. We simply didn't have the capacity for this kind of commitment. The collateral damage in other places in our lives would be significant. When I went to Karen about my change of mind, before I could get the words out of my mouth, she blurted out, "We can't do this." All of a sudden we had clarity; I called the county and declined.

A week later, Karen fell and broke her back. She was in the hospital for a week and then confined to a bed for a while after that. And at some point in all of the chaos of that emergency I remember thinking, "Thank the Lord we don't have an autistic foster child living with us right now." If he had been placed with us, he almost certainly would have had to endure the trauma of being moved to another home as Karen recuperated. It seems clear to me that the Lord saved us (and that child) from a terrible situation.

So, how do we know where to draw the lines when it comes to serving difficult people in difficult places? Given that the needs are endless and the call to sacrifice is extreme, when is it ever okay to decline an opportunity to serve? How should you be working to see the gospel spread among the needy people in your community? Should you go and seek out opportunities in other places? The answers to these kinds of questions may not be easy and obvious, but here are four principles that can help guide us as we make decisions.

Principle 1:
God Doesn't Need You

One of the things that distinguishes the true God of the universe from the idols of the nations is his self-sufficiency. The idols of the nations are utterly impotent (Ps. 115:4–7). They need to be carried around by their makers (Isa. 46:7). But there is something about the human condition that prefers a god like this. We like to have control. We like to think that God needs us or is indebted to us or that we can manipulate him by our behavior. But in his message to the Athenians, the apostle Paul corrects this misunderstanding of God's nature: "The God who made the world and everything in it, being Lord of heaven and earth, does not live in temples made by man, nor is he served by human hands, as though he needed anything, since he himself gives to all mankind life and breath and everything" (Acts 17:24–25).

What Paul is saying is of the utmost importance, especially to someone thinking through ministry to the poor. The true God of the universe is independent; he does not need anything, including your service or mine. So we need it settled in our minds from the outset that while God may choose to employ us to accomplish his purposes, the spread of the gospel among the poor never depends finally on us.

The hard places in your world do not need you to be their savior; God has already provided them with one. God does not send his people into ministry situations because he is unable to do the work himself. Rather, he has generously chosen to bless us by giving us the opportunity to do ministry among the poor. We have the privilege of participating in the work that God is doing in the world.

If you do not take hold of this truth up front, you are more likely to burn out or become bitter when you do not see immediate fruit from your labors or when people do not appreciate what you are doing for them. If you put the burden of saving people on yourself, you will quickly find that you are not up to the task. If you imagine that the God of heaven is wringing his hands, really hoping that you pull it together and get the job done, then your failures threaten to crush you and your apparent successes will lead you into pride.

Principle 2:
All Christian Discipleship Has a Cost

Jesus said some things that sound sweet and loving to our ears—things like "love your neighbor" and "do unto others as you would have them do unto you." That's a religion that most people agree sounds right. We may move toward ministry among the poor based on those kinds of commands, and that's fine as far as it goes.

But Jesus also said some things that were genuinely radical, things that alienated much of his audience and painted an extreme picture of what it means to follow him. Look at just three examples from Luke's Gospel:

> And he said to all, "If anyone would come after me, let him deny himself and take up his cross daily and follow me. For whoever would save his life will lose it, but whoever loses his life for my sake will save it. For what does it profit a man

if he gains the whole world and loses or forfeits himself?" (Luke 9:23–25)

As they were going along the road, someone said to him, "I will follow you wherever you go." And Jesus said to him, "Foxes have holes, and birds of the air have nests, but the Son of Man has nowhere to lay his head." To another he said, "Follow me." But he said, "Lord, let me first go and bury my father." And Jesus said to him, "Leave the dead to bury their own dead. But as for you, go and proclaim the kingdom of God." Yet another said, "I will follow you, Lord, but let me first say farewell to those at my home." Jesus said to him, "No one who puts his hand to the plow and looks back is fit for the kingdom of God." (Luke 9:57–62)

Now great crowds accompanied him, and he turned and said to them, "If anyone comes to me and does not hate his own father and mother and wife and children and brothers and sisters, yes, and even his own life, he cannot be my disciple." (Luke 14:25–26)

We could say many things about these passages, but for our purposes it is important to note the larger picture that Jesus is painting: being his disciple is costly. There is not a "no sacrifice" plan that you can sign up for. If you are going to follow Jesus, then you are getting on board to serve him no matter what the cost. If Jesus is Lord, then he must be the controlling principle in all of our plans and decisions. To put it bluntly, this means that we don't get to say "no" just because ministry to the poor might be costly or scary. Following Jesus means that we might lose our lives, and anyone who is unwilling is unfit to be his disciple.

This truth has been understood by generations of missionaries who have taken the gospel to dangerous places. This truth undergirds them as they bury their spouses and their children on the mission field. This truth comforts them as they give up their own lives. This truth confronts us, particularly as we think about the impact that working with needy people might have on our families. No part of our lives is off-limits to Jesus. Nothing is "ours" in an ultimate sense. So what would your life and your obedience to Christ look like if you weren't afraid of what you might lose?

I can hear the objection: "But as a parent, my first priority is to evangelize and disciple my children! It sounds like you are saying that I should take time and energy away from that task." Yes, and, well, yes. Parents must evangelize and disciple their children. But could it be that the most evangelistically effective thing a mother or father could do is to show their children that Jesus is the greatest treasure there is? Perhaps part of being a good parent is showing a child that though he or she is dearly loved, he or she is not the best thing in the world; Jesus is. By living a life of sacrifice in front of our children, we show them the shape of Christian discipleship. If we never sacrifice or embrace a difficult situation for fear that it might cost our children something, we show them that whatever we might say with our lips, they, not Jesus, are our highest priority.

Certainly, wisdom is called for here. I am most certainly not encouraging men to spend endless hours away from their wives and children—"But it's for the sake of ministry, family!" How many wives and children of Christian leaders have grown bitter toward the faith because a husband or father seemed to care more about ministry than them?

Also, I am not saying that sacrifice is an end unto itself. The goal is not to find the most sacrificial thing to do and then do it. We are not all called to pack our bags and take our family open-air preaching in Pyongyang. There is little virtue in embracing danger or pain or sacrifice for its own sake.

But for most of us, that is not the cliff we are likely to fall off. As a pastor, I do not suffer from an overwhelming stream of church members who are sacrificing too much. Instead, many of us are tempted to make our children into idols, putting their comfort and desires far above those of Jesus.

To be clear, then, I'm not calling for a "balance" between work and ministry. I'm calling you to give yourself wholly to the ministry, and to give yourself wholly to your family, and to let your wife and children experience both *with* you. And usually this means they will need to sacrifice some of what this world says they are entitled to have.

Principle 3:
Not All Sacrifice Is Strategic

As we've said, it can be hard to know what we are supposed to do in a given situation. There is a temptation (admittedly, one that I love to encounter in my congregation) to take Jesus's portrait of extreme discipleship and seek to obey it in extreme ways. And while that may be a good idea from time to time and there may be lots of good motivations wrapped up in that impulse, sometimes Christians don't think clearly about the ways they can best invest their lives in the spread of the gospel.

Let me show you what I mean. Take two members of a church:

- Charles is a technology nerd. He makes a lot of money as a software developer, but he is more than a little awkward in social situations. He is a kind person, but is shy and tends to say the wrong thing when he gets nervous.
- Linda is a grocery store clerk. She is just able to eke out a living for herself and her two children, but she is a very fruitful evangelist. She has a knack for building relationships with unbelievers and turning conversations to Christ. She seems to attract needy people.

Now let's say that one Sunday in church both Charles and Linda hear a great sermon about the cost of discipleship. They are both convinced that the Lord would have them invest more of their lives in seeing the gospel spread among the poor and needy in their area. And so Charles decides to quit his job and start teaching at a school in an impoverished neighborhood his church is trying to reach with the gospel. Linda decides that she should start working double shifts at the store so that she can have extra money to give away to the poor.

What's wrong with that picture? Both Christians are living in a radical way; both have responded to the extreme call to discipleship with an act of obedience. But it's not clear that either Charles or Linda is acting wisely. They are sacrificing, but they are not necessarily sacrificing strategically. They are not taking into consideration how the Lord has made them, what he has gifted them to do, and how they might most effectively bring those things to bear for the purpose of spreading the gospel among the needy.

Charles is really good at making money. So while he should be working to be a better evangelist, he may be best positioned to use his gifts to help finance the spread of the gospel and the relief of the poor. Linda, on the other hand, is really good at connecting with people. So while she should be thinking about ways that her family might be able to give more money for gospel purposes, her time is not *best* sacrificed by working longer hours at minimum wage. Instead, she might look for ways to free up time to be around needy people in her area.

This is where involvement in a local church is important. In a church, there will be a variety of gifts, strengths, obligations, and resources. Working together, churches can think about how everyone best fits into the bigger picture and might sacrificially deploy their God-given gifts to help see their community reached with the gospel.

Principle 4:
Sacrifice and Service Is the Path to Final Joy

Think about what happens when someone invests his or her money in the stock market. This person takes a resource that he has (say, $1,000), and he sacrifices all of the ways that he could enjoy it in the short-term (say, buy a lot of tacos, or all the latest video games, or nice clothes). Instead of "cashing in" all the benefits the $1,000 could buy now, he invests that money in the hope of a greater resource in the future (say, $1,500 in ten years).

In the same way, a Christian is called to invest his life on this earth. We have resources (time, skill, money) that we can use to bring ourselves comfort and pleasure now, or we can invest them in the cause of Jesus. Now, it may not be worth waiting ten years for a $500 return on investment, but ask yourself: do you think it's worth investing everything you have in the work of Christ? Does he offer a good return on investment? To answer that question, look at the conversation that we read about in Matthew 19:

> Then Peter said in reply, "See, we have left everything and followed you. What then will we have?" Jesus said to them, "Truly, I say to you, in the new world, when the Son of Man will sit on his glorious throne, you who have followed me will also sit on twelve thrones, judging the twelve tribes of Israel. And everyone who has left houses or brothers or sisters or father or mother or children or lands, for my name's sake, will receive a hundredfold and will inherit eternal life." (Matt. 19:27–29)

Peter left everything to follow Jesus. You can understand why he might be nervous, looking for clarification. So Jesus affirms that in fact Peter had invested wisely. The sacrifice of possessions and real estate and family will yield a tremendous eternal return on investment.

If you could go back in time and buy stock in a company like Apple or Google, you would be crazy not to. It's a sure thing; it's a "can't lose" stock. In fact, you'd be nuts not to liquidate every asset that you had in order to invest as much as you possibly could in one of those companies. In the same way, we should invest everything we have for the sake of Jesus's name. There is an amazing, guaranteed return on your investment!

Conclusion

So back to the question that we asked at the outset of this chapter: given that the opportunities and needs are limitless, how do we know what we should do and what we shouldn't do? There are no easy answers. We have to examine our hearts and know where we are prone to fear, selfishness, and indifference. We also have to be on guard against pride and against the desire to earn our salvation through works of service. We also would be wise to consider our service in light of our role in the wider ministry of our local church. But in the end, the question is not whether discipleship will come with a cost (it will), but how we can best invest our lives in Christ's kingdom? Do you not think the reward is worth our entire lives? Is the kingdom of God in hard places not a pearl of infinite price—worth selling everything to buy?

General Index

Scripture Index

2✝schemes

Gospel Churches for Scotland's Poorest

20schemes exists to bring gospel hope to Scotland's poorest communities through the revitalization and planting of healthy, gospel-preaching churches, ultimately led by a future generation of indigenous church leaders.

> *"If we are really going to see a turnaround in the lives of residents in our poorest communities, then we have to embrace a radical and long-term strategy which will bring gospel-hope to untold thousands."*
>
> **MEZ MCCONNELL,** Ministry Director

We believe that building healthy churches in Scotland's poorest communities will bring true, sustainable, and long-term renewal to countless lives.

THE NEED IS URGENT

Learn more about our work and how to partner with us at:

20SCHEMES.COM
TWITTER.COM/20SCHEMES
FACEBOOK.COM/20SCHEMES
INSTAGRAM.COM/20SCHEMES

Building Healthy Churches

9Marks exists to equip church leaders with a biblical vision and practical resources for displaying God's glory to the nations through healthy churches.

To that end, we want to see churches characterized by these nine marks of health:

1   Expositional Preaching
2   Biblical Theology
3   A Biblical Understanding of the Gospel
4   A Biblical Understanding of Conversion
5   A Biblical Understanding of Evangelism
6   Biblical Church Membership
7   Biblical Church Discipline
8   Biblical Discipleship
9   Biblical Church Leadership

Find all our Crossway titles
and other resources at
www.9Marks.org